AF271456

The Rolls-Royce and Bentley
Volume 2: Coachbuilt models
1945 to 1985

The Rolls-Royce and Bentley

Volume 2: Coachbuilt models
1945 to 1985

A collector's guide
by Graham Robson

MOTOR RACING PUBLICATIONS LTD
Unit 6, The Pilton Estate, 46 Pitlake, Croydon CR0 3RY, England

ISBN 0 900549 87 4
First published 1984
Reprinted 1987
Reprinted 1989

Copyright © 1984 — Graham Robson and Motor Racing Publications Ltd

All rights reserved. No part of this publication may be reproduced,
stored in a retrieval system, or transmitted, in any form or by any
means, electronic, mechanical, photocopying, recording or otherwise,
without the prior permission of Motor Racing Publications Ltd

Photosetting by Zee Creative Ltd., London SW16
Printed in Great Britain by The Amadeus Press,
Huddersfield

Contents

Introduction

For 20 years after the end of the Second World War, Rolls-Royce Ltd based the design of all its private cars on just two generations of chassis and two types of engines. Much is known about some of them, and little about others. It was for that reason that MRP and the author decided to tackle a detailed survey of the 'separate-chassis cars from Crewe' — Bentley and Rolls-Royce, Mk VI, Silver Dawn, Silver Cloud, Silver Wraith, Phantom, Continental and the like.

It has been a complex task, not because the facts are difficult to assemble (every reference item, in fact, is readily available), but because there are so many of them. For that reason, I hope, the reader will immediately realize that this, and its companion volume on the 'standard-steel' cars, is not merely 'yet another Rolls-Royce book'.

One reason — the main reason, in fact — for covering all the separate-chassis cars at the same time is that they are all related in certain ways. In the past, several fine books have been written about certain models, but very little about others, and most have concentrated on the cars' styling, the quality of their construction and their character, along with the aura and the personalities surrounding them.

For my part, I have decided to cover fine machines like the Rolls-Royce Silver Wraith and the Bentley R-Type Continental as cars — not as talismans, status symbols, or deities to be worshipped. It is, in other words, something of a 'nuts and bolts' study, as all previous *Collector's Guides* have been, and — more than many previous books on the Rolls-Royce and Bentley marques — it also sets out to cross-refer one model and its 'building block' engineering to another.

When John Blunsden and I sat down to work out a framework for this book, it was immediately clear that 20 years' worth of series-production 'standard-steel' cars, and no less than 38 years' worth of special coachbuilt car production, would provide far too much fact, and need too many illustrations, for all the cars to be covered in one volume. Accordingly, we hope we have achieved justice by splitting the work into two companion volumes — this one dealing with the models always provided with special coachwork, and the other with what are popularly known as the 'standard-steel' saloons.

In places, therefore, certain features of one model may have been summarized, while cross-referring to the other volume. My apologies for that, but I wanted to avoid repetition wherever possible.

Although the sub-derivatives allow the descriptive material to be split into many sections, I really only have to cover two basic models, all built at Crewe between 1945 and the mid-1980s. The Bentley Mk VI type of chassis was also that used, in principle, under the Silver Wraith, the Phantom IV and, of course, the Bentley R-Type Continentals. To follow it, there was the Rolls-Royce Silver Cloud/Bentley S-Series chassis, from which the Phantom V and VI chassis evolved and has been in production (albeit very limited in recent years) for 25 years.

This book, however, is more factual than philosophical. It is neither an essay in character assassination, nor an attempt to write descriptive purple prose. It neither rubbishes the cars for being demonstrably behind the engineering times for some years (drum brakes when the rest of the world was going disc, separate frame when most other marques were going monocoque), nor does it hide the known facts behind clouds of rhetoric about radiator shapes or detail equipment.

It is, in short, a factual story of what these cars were, and are, all about. I thought it important to detail how and when the major changes were phased in, and I thought it important to try to tell newcomers to the marques (you would be surprised — there are still thousands of them out there!) how the one related to the other. In terms of the what, the when, and the how, there are even some surprises!

Nevertheless, it is worth recalling that for years Rolls-Royce Ltd felt able to advertise their machines as 'The Best Car in the World'. I do not believe, for one moment, that they were exaggerating, even if 'The Best' usually referred more to quality of materials and of construction than to quality of technical layout. 'The Best', in the Robotham/Grylls context, was obviously not a fixed standard, for this is a near-40-year story of continuous change and improvement.

Out there, do you have a Silver Wraith with a 4.9-litre engine, a Phantom IV of any type, or a coachbuilt long-wheelbase Silver Cloud I? If you do, or if you merely want to know how rare it is, read on!

GRAHAM ROBSON

Acknowledgements

Even when tackling a factual book about Rolls-Royce and Bentley, I found that by no means all the material I needed was instantly available. Accordingly, I had to rely on help for a variety of sources to fill in all the gaps in my knowledge.

Where to start? Without a doubt, by expressing my grateful thanks to Colonel Eric Barrass, genial secretary of the Rolls-Royce Enthusiasts' Club, not only for his encouragement, but for paving the way for me to visit The Hunt House, in Paulerspury, where the most amazingly detailed archive is maintained; to Mrs King, at The Hunt House, for showing me the ropes and answering my questions; to David Preston and Mike Weatherby, of Rolls-Royce Motors Ltd. for their help in tracing Phantom VI statistics, also for supplying a good selection of photographs, to Bentley archivist extraordinaire Stanley Sedgwick, who effectively saved me half the research by already having done it for his Bentley members!; to Mirco Decet, for loaning me many photographs, many of which have been used in these two volumes; to Ray Hedley, for supplying several interesting photographs from a recent gathering at Duxford; to my publisher, John Blunsden, also for providing a big choice of archive pictures, which have proved to be invaluable; to *Autocar* and its Editor, Ray Hutton, and to *Thoroughbred & Classic Cars*, its Editor, Tony Dron, and its Associate Editor, Lionel Burrell, not only for being the best magazines of their kind in the business and amazingly fruitful sources of research material, but for allowing me to comb their back numbers and lift some of the comment and performance figures. Also to Tony Curtis, of *Motor*, for a set of Phantom V performance figures; but especially to my old colleague Warren Allport, not this time in his capacity as *Autocar's* Assistant Editor, but because he is acknowledged as one of *the* leading Rolls-Royce/Bentley experts in the media. Warren not only put me straight on several points (will we ever locate that missing wheelbase inch, I wonder?), but took the trouble to read the manuscripts of both volumes, and commented on everything. For years I have been telling Warren to write this book himself — at least, I hope my own efforts now carry the stamp of his approval.

GRAHAM ROBSON

The epitome of dignified and luxurious Rolls-Royce ownership and travel. The rear compartment of a Phantom V from H.J. Mulliner, Park Ward. A picture taken shortly before cocktail time, no doubt.

CHAPTER 1

Ancestors and heritage

The great coachbuilding traditions

As another of my contemporaries has already pointed out: 'Coachbuilding was already well-developed when the Roman bloods drove their richly decorated chariots through the streets of Rome.' How true. He also made the point that the first British-built coach was not ordered until the mid-16th century, after which this craftsman's art spread rapidly.

As far as Rolls-Royce and Bentley cars are concerned, their early bodies were *always* coachbuilt — Rolls-Royce from 1904 and Bentley from 1919 — though British coachbuilders were already at the peak of their reputation before then. It was not merely that the two marques independently decided to patronize coachbuilders, but that they had no choice in the matter. Until private car production was resumed after the end of the Second World War, Rolls-Royce and Bentley had never produced their own bodywork, nor even had a body engineering department.

Indeed, it was not until quantity-production manufacturers like Wolseley and Austin expanded that 'in-house' bodyshells began to be produced. At the very beginning of the age of motoring (and that is nearly 100 years ago as these words are being written), all motor car manufacturers produced self-contained rolling chassis and a specialist coachbuilder then produced the bodywork. Even in the 1920s, many sizeable concerns still confined themselves to building rolling chassis, though more and more of them were adopting an approved coachbuilder with whom to place much of their business.

At a time when wage levels were relatively low and the supply of skilled carpenters, metalworkers and trimmers was still abundant, it made economic sense for a company like Rolls-Royce or Bentley to allow their customers to choose a body style and have it built to their requirements. In other words, it might not have been any cheaper for the chassis manufacturer to do the job 'in house', and it would certainly not have been feasible to offer as much choice. The coachbuilders, too, with modest premises and little capital equipment, could remain profitable at a very leisurely rate of production.

Even though times and social niceties were changing all the time, the great coachbuilding traditions were alive, well and mostly profitable in the mid-1930s. To take 1935 as an example — the year, in fact, in which the V12-engined Rolls-Royce Phantom III was revealed — *The Autocar's* Olympia motor show number listed no fewer than 42 coachbuilders' displays. Rolls-Royce or Bentley chassis were featured on 15 of them, and all the great names such as H.J. Mulliner, Park Ward, James Young, Rippon and Windovers were represented.

One of the problems of building cars in this way was that it tended to take a great deal of time. I once knew an elderly Yorkshire businessman who finally aspired to Rolls-Royce ownership, late in life. He walked on to the stand of a specialist coachbuilder and demanded to buy *that* car, right there and then, and 'would you like cash or a cheque, lad? The salesman had to assure him that one just didn't buy exclusive cars like that, that he might get one within a year, and that details should be discussed. 'Nay, lad', said the woolman, who was of an age which expected instant obedience: 'I'm old now, and I'll be older then. In fact, I might be dead. I want it now!'

A seasoned Rolls-Royce or Bentley buyer would have known

Well before Bentley was owned by Rolls-Royce, the company built big and impressive machines at Cricklewood, in North London. This was an example of W.O.'s masterpiece, the six-cylinder overhead-camshaft 6½-litre engine of the late 1920s.

better, and would have laid his plans accordingly. Choosing the chassis would have been easy enough (and the chauffeur was often asked to advise), but the choice of body styles was vast. Consultations with the factory might lead to a coachbuilder ever so discreetly being recommended (or even, at times, not recommended). Discussions as to the styling, the details and the fittings would be long and painstaking — after which the chosen bodyshell would slowly, carefully and infinitely satisfyingly begin to take shape.

In the more leisured days of the 1920s and the 1930s it was nothing for a new car to be ordered at one Olympia motor show, but not to be ready before the following summer. It took patience, as well as money, to buy a coachbuilt Bentley or Rolls-Royce!

However, as already explained in some detail in Volume 1 of this study, Rolls-Royce detected a definite fall in the demand for their coachbuilt cars towards the end of the 1930s, even though they tried all logical ways to cut down on complication and on the

delay between orders being placed and delivery being effected. Although we must not be bamboozled by figures alone (especially as the Derby works was turning itself more and more towards the production of aero-engines for military use in the frantic rearmament drive), it is a fact that Rolls-Royce chassis production dwindled from its traditional 1,500 cars a year in the mid-1930s to a mere 597 in 1938 and less than 400 in the first eight months of 1939.

Faced with such a decline in business, the coachbuilders who had previously relied on companies like Rolls-Royce, Daimler and — to a lesser extent — Armstrong-Siddeley, Lagonda, Alvis and the like — were forced to contract their businesses, rationalize their custom-built offerings, or even go out of business.

The wisest concerns began, covertly and very discreetly, to standardize in many ways. At first this process was confined to detail, but later in the 1930s it had progressed to much larger hidden sub-assemblies, and sometimes even complete body

Rumour has it that Rolls-Royce were determined to buy up Bentley to kill off competition from the splendid new 8-litre model. Looking at this big saloon, one can see why!

The 'Derby' Bentleys of the mid-1930s were elegant, fast, sports saloons, advertised by Rolls-Royce as the 'Silent Sports Car'. This 3½-litre had a Park Ward bodyshell.

Park Ward produced this graceful coachbuilt style for the Rolls-Royce 40/50hp Phantom II Continental chassis in the 1930s.

The most complex pre-1939 Rolls-Royce was the V12-engined Phantom III. This example, with a Park Ward 'Sports Limousine' bodyshell, could be owner-driven or chauffeur-driven, according to the lucky owner's wishes.

Wraiths were only built in 1938 and 1939, but sold well, even though many of them had rather formal body styles, like this Park Ward example.

The independent front suspension of the Wraith had semi-trailing wishbones and a horizontally positioned coil spring enclosed in an oil bath, quite different from that of the postwar cars.

frames. Before the onset of the Hitler war, it was often possible for Park Ward (for instance) to offer a more or less standard body style, capable of clever disguise by external changes. Park Ward, indeed, was one of the most forward-thinking constructors, and in 1935 they patented an all-steel method of body framing to replace the use of seasoned woods.

The beginning of the end for the bespoke bodybuilding traditions was signalled in 1937. By this time Thrupp & Maberly had already become beholden to the Rootes Group, but it was the year in which Hooper took over the ailing Barker & Co (Coachbuilders) Ltd. Two years later, to secure their lines for the future, Rolls-Royce annexed Park Ward, which became a wholly owned subsidiary. Even before this time, however, Park Ward had been one of no more than three or four 'favoured' coachbuilders, regularly getting clearance from the factory to lay down up to 25 at a time of their latest standardized sports saloons or drophead coupes.

The truly top-drawer Rolls-Royce models, however, continued to rise above all this commercial juggling for survival, and to the respectful general public it looked as if things were

The 'Paulin' or 'Embiricos' Bentley of 1938-39 was the inspirational ancestor to the R-Type Continental and had astonishingly advanced styling for the period. The car survives to this day.

going on, and would continue to do so, very much as always. During the 1920s, there had been two chassis on offer — the 20hp and the 40/50hp types — and by the early 1930s these had evolved into the 20/25 and the 40/50 Phantom II.

Following Rolls-Royce's purchase of the assets of Bentley at the end of 1931, a new Bentley range (really yet another type of Rolls-Royce, smaller and faster than the 20/25hp from which it evolved) was also developed. From 1938, therefore, no fewer than three different chassis were being produced at Derby, all in strictly limited quantities. First, there was the latest Bentley, the $4\frac{1}{4}$-litre, which had an overhead-valve engine, a 10ft 6in

wheelbase and beam axles at front and rear. Then there was the newly announced Rolls-Royce Wraith (*not* the Silver Wraith, please note), with a different version of the $4\frac{1}{4}$-litre 'six', a wheelbase of 11ft 4in, wider wheel tracks and independent front suspension. Finally, there was the massive and complex Rolls-Royce Phantom III, with an 11ft 10in wheelbase, coil-spring independent front suspension (different in much detail from the Wraith), even wider wheel tracks and a 7.3-litre V12 engine.

In the meantime, W.A. Robotham, development chief of the car division, had been recommending the setting-up of a programme of new rationalized models for some time, and by

Rolls-Royce produced this four-door prototype, called a Bentley Corniche, just before the Second World War, effectively as a more practical alternative to the 'Paulin' Bentley. Not the prettiest of styles, it was broken up before the war years.

1939 this policy had been approved and work put in hand to carry it out. But it all depended on what was meant by 'rationalization', for the same new basic chassis design was to have a variety of wheelbases, there were to be new four-cylinder, six-cylinder *and* eight-cylinder engines, some models would have standardized bodies, and some coachbuilt bodyshells.

Then, on September 1, 1939, Germany's armies marched into Poland and the onset of the Second World War was inevitable. Within days, Rolls-Royce Ltd closed down the production of private-car chassis at Derby, a process which would never be reversed. Six years of war, grievous loss of life, and a revolution in social conditions (not to mention political and financial upheaval) all meant that the future climate for Rolls-Royce would be very different indeed.

CHAPTER 2

Rolls-Royce Silver Wraith

Luxury in an austere world

Is it an exaggeration to suggest that without the Rolls-Royce Merlin aero-engine Britain might have been defeated in the Second World War, in 1940? That's debatable, even today — but there is no doubt that the Merlin was a magnificent engine, and that for years Rolls-Royce strained every sinew to build more and more, increasingly powerful, derivatives. The Merlin was to be built in several factories, one of which was a new building in Pyms Lane, Crewe. Only 256 Merlins were made at Crewe in 1939, but no fewer than 6,116 flooded out of the gates in 1943. Well before the war was won, Rolls-Royce had decided to move the centre of their motor car production facilities to Crewe, leaving Derby entirely devoted to aero-engine production.

Even while management and workforce were slogging away, six and sometimes seven days a week, on the war effort, there was still time for personalities like Ernest Hives, A.G. Elliott and W.A. Robotham to think deeply about the future of the car division. As I have recounted in more detail in Volume 1, the decline in Rolls-Royce car production in the late 1930s, and the increasing scarcity of demand for specialized coachwork, had led the company to sketch out a new 'standardization' policy.

According to Robotham, in his autobiography *Silver Ghost and Silver Dawn*, not only was a rationalized range of four-cylinder, six-cylinder and eight-cylinder engines laid down, all of which would share the same bore and stroke, pistons, connecting rods, valve gear and many of the machine shop facilities, but thought was given to a range of rationalized chassis to accept these. By the end of the 1930s, it had been decided to expand production and to replace the Phantom III, Wraith and 4¼-litre Bentley models by the following cars:

Silver Phantom	8-cylinder engine, to succeed Phantom III
Silver Wraith	6-cylinder engine, to succeed Wraith
Bentley Mk V	to succeed the 4¼-litre Bentley
Silver Dawn	Bentley MK V, with Rolls-Royce radiator,
Silver Ripple	8-cylinder engine in 4¼-litre chassis, known as 'Scalded Cat'

The Bentley Mk V, of which only 14 cars were built at or around the outbreak of war, was the first rationalized car to be seen in public, though its engine was of the existing 4¼-litre Bentley type, with conventional overhead valve gear.

These plans, of course, were overtaken by events, but the rationalized B-Series range of engines was thoroughly developed during the war years, and some prototype cars covered many tens of thousands of miles on official business. I have already covered the thinking behind the engine design in Volume 1, particularly the decision to retain existing bore and stroke dimensions and same cylinder spacing, all to allow existing machine tools to be used.

At this point, however, I can do no better than quote Robotham's own words about future events, and how it came to pass that one coachbuilt Rolls-Royce chassis and one very similar Bentley with a 'standard-steel' bodyshell were put into production:

'In the autumn of 1944, our situation . . . was very satisfactory for we had an up-to-date design for a range of chassis . . . On the body side, however, we had no progress at all, and it was clear that not only would coachbuilt bodies made in the prewar manner be doubtful in quality, but they would also be

The original Rolls-Royce Silver Wraith chassis of 1946, backed by a very un-Rolls-Royce-like cloth! Its wheelbase was 10ft 7in, 7 inches longer than that of the Bentley Mk VI, the difference really being accommodated in the centre of the cruciform.

For many years, all coachbuilt body styles were drawn out, full-size, so that the coachbuilders could then construct template shapes from which to build the bodies. This shot was taken at James Young, in Bromley.

prohibitively expensive.

'Furthermore, it seemed improbable that more than 60 per cent of the ageing craftsmen who could build one-off bodies would have survived five years of war. As a result, we should not get the quantity of bodies necessary for us to build an economic number of chassis annually.'

Accordingly, the top-level decision was taken that Rolls-Royce Ltd would commission the tooling of a 'standard-steel' body style (from the Pressed Steel Company, of Cowley), that they would begin by badging this as a Bentley, just in case the traditional type of Rolls-Royce customer would be offended by having to accept the same style as everyone else, and that there would also be a single postwar Rolls-Royce model which, as always, would be constructed up to the self-contained rolling-chassis stage, then delivered to a coachbuilder for completion by traditional methods. This became the Silver Wraith, which made its public bow in April 1946.

This new car, incidentally, was the first production Rolls-Royce officially to carry the 'Silver . . .' name in its title, for although many people call the 1906-1925 models 'Silver Ghosts', they are more properly known as 40/50 models, with 'Silver Ghost' being applied only to the famous single example, registered AX 201, which is now owned by Rolls-Royce Motors Ltd.

According to the plans laid towards the end of the 1930s, the Silver Wraith was to replace the short-lived Wraith, and so it did, though because no successor to the very large and costly Phantom III came along at once, it also took on the mantle of the

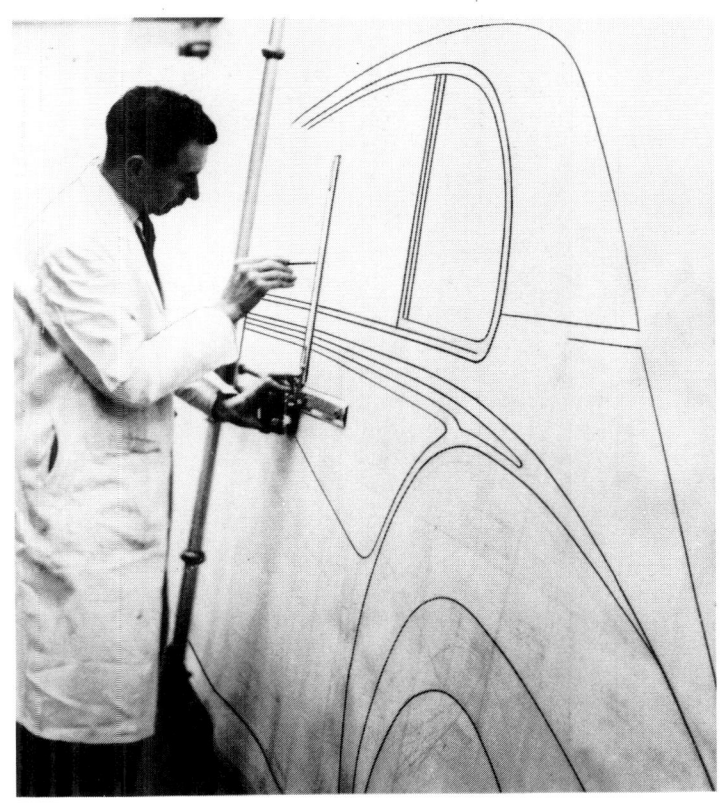

This James Young Silver Wraith saloon dates from 1947 — there are touches of the 'standard-steel' saloon around the rear quarters of the elegant body.

largest Rolls-Royce of the period. Such were the signs of progress, even at Rolls-Royce, that the Silver Wraith had a significantly shorter wheelbase (10ft 7in, compared with 11ft 4in), though it was certainly no lighter, and did not appear to offer any less space inside a typical limousine bodyshell.

In accordance with the strategy agreed some years previously, the rolling chassis of this new Rolls-Royce was to the same *general* design as that of the new standard-bodied Bentley, though there were several detail differences, notably to the wheelbase and the engine tune.

Both the Mk VI Bentley and the Silver Wraith chassis were identical in layout to the first of the 'rationalized' chassis, that of the Mk V Bentley. Just to show that rationalization was carried only so far, and not all the way, I should also point out the Mk V's wheelbase was different yet again! For the record, the figures were: Mk V 10ft 4in, Mk VI 10ft 0in and Silver Wraith 10ft 7in.

Front suspension, by coil springs, wishbones and an anti-roll torsion bar, also featured lever-arm dampers, where the lever arms also doubled as top wishbones in the overall suspension geometry, and while this was the same as that used on the 1939 Mk V and the 1946 Mk VI, it was entirely different from that used on the prewar Wraiths and Phantom IIIs (which were the first Rolls-Royce cars to used independent front suspension). On the new cars the coil springs were vertical and exposed, and the wishbones were angled somewhat forwards (from the inboard towards the outboard pivots), whereas on the prewar cars the springs were horizontal, enclosed in an oil bath, with the dampers also included in the same 'pod', and the wishbones 'trailed' significantly. As before, on Mk V and Mk VI Bentleys, the damper settings were fixed, not instantly adjustable from the driving seat.

Rear suspension was also 'as Mk V/Mk VI', with a hypoid-bevel rear axle located by gaitered half-elliptic leaf springs, but no anti-roll bar, and with hydraulic lever-arm dampers, adjustable for stiffness by the driver from a small lever mounted on the steering wheel boss. Steering was by Marles cam and

A majestic-looking Silver Wraith touring limousine by H.J. Mulliner, complete with two-tone paintwork.

This Silver Wraith drophead coupe, by James Young, was a very enduring design. Note the rear wheel cover carrying the 'RR' monogram.

roller, with a rather complex linkage to the wheels featuring a central pivot hidden inside the chassis cross-member.

The frame itself was a rigid assembly of pressings, some rivetted, some welded together, with channel-section side members and a massive cruciform member which effectively linked the front passenger bulkhead to the sweep over the back axle. Wheelbase difference between the three types was accommodated at the centre — really at the 'X' section of the cruciform, where the Mk VI had eight rivets down each side of the bracing plates and the Silver Wraith had 10.

The Silver Wraith's brakes, part Girling and part Lockheed, but built to Rolls-Royce standards, were the same as those fitted to the Mk VI, with 12.25 × 2.6in front and rear drums, along with the familiar well-developed mechanical servo mechanism (as inspired by that first fitted to a Hispano-Suiza model), mounted to the right of the gearbox casing. Front operation was hydraulic and rear mechanical, an arrangement partly dictated by the use of the unique servo and the needs of the handbrake linkage.

Similar steel wheels to the Mk VI were also used, though two types and sizes of tyres were chosen from time to time — 7.00-16in or 6.50-17in — to support the extra weight of special coachwork.

Although the Silver Wraith's engine carried the familiar engine capacity of 4,257cc and the same bore and stroke, it was an entirely different unit in almost every way from the 25/30hp and Wraith engines used in the 1930s. Also to be found in the Mk VI Bentley, and in the Silver Dawn which would follow three years hence, the new unit was a B60 design, one of three rationalized layouts developed just before the outbreak of war, and thoroughly proved throughout that conflict. I have already described this engine in some detail in Volume 1, but for this application, I should mention that there was a single downdraught Stromberg carburettor — which did not allow as much power to be developed as the twin SUs used in the Mk VI Bentley, but provided more consistent slow running and a more docile response at those speeds. Although Rolls-Royce did not officially state the peak power output of this fine new engine, which breathed very well, thanks to the use of overhead inlet, but side exhaust valves, *The Autocar* was allowed to mention in its

. . . and great minds obviously think alike because this is a very similar 1952 style by Freestone & Webb!

Even by 1947, Hooper had evolved this very smart touring limousine style for the Silver Wraith with those characteristic rear quarters.

The chassis is Silver Wraith, but the sports saloon coachwork is by Vincents of Reading — a real rarity for 1952.

technical analysis of April 5 1946 that: 'The new Silver Wraith six-cylinder engine develops about 137bhp with open exhaust on the test-bed, and about 122bhp as installed and silenced in the car.' Later, in 1950, when *Commercial Motor* described the B-Series engines, it quoted 126bhp at 3,750rpm for the same derivative, coupled with the huge torque figure of 227lb/ft at 1,800rpm.

Backing the new engine was the much revised type of four-speed synchromesh gearbox first seen in the Bentley Mk V in 1939, in which there was no synchromesh on first gear, the mechanical servo was driven from the output shaft, and there was a right-hand gear-change, the lever of which was placed in a visible 'gate' outboard of the driver's seat. All of this was good traditional stuff, and no-one was complaining, but eyebrows *were* raised somewhat when it was noticed that there was an 'umbrella' type of handbrake lever mounted under the facia, alongside the steering column.

At the rear, the hypoid rear axle was the same as that of the 1939 Bentley Mk V and postwar Mk VI, with the same 3.727:1

final-drive ratio as the Mk VI and the proposed 'Corniche' of 1939; the Mk V's ratio had been 4.3:1, with an overdrive feature on top. As ever on coachbuilt Rolls-Royces, the fuel tank (18 Imperial gallons in this case) was tucked down behind the rear axle, between the side members, with the filler neck on the left side. An owner-driver, no doubt, might have been horrified to find the 12-volt battery tucked down under the floor, actually under the driver's seat, but once again this was the 'rationalized' position, and at least it made a change from being under the *rear* seat, as on the 1938 Wraith!

Naturally, too, there were permanently fitted hydraulic jacks and centralized chassis lubrication, which was only to be expected on such a vehicle, and in spite of the very straitened times in which Rolls-Royce, and indeed the entire country, found itself, construction was to the very highest, painstaking standards. *The Autocar* opened its description by gushing: 'All the world knows that Rolls-Royce carry on an unremitting search for engineering perfection in everything they undertake', though they also went on to mention the new policy of

Three views of the rather unwieldy attempt by Park Ward to produce an attractive 'straight-through' wing line on the Silver Wraith in 1948.

H.J. Mulliner always had a sure touch with limousine bodies on the Silver Wraith. This car dates from the early 1950s.

standardization. In addition, it was stated: 'The engines have been used [during the war] not only in cars, but in buses and carriers as well. Nearly a million miles have been covered, including 26,000 miles on European autobahns before the war.'

The new Silver Wraith chassis, in other words, were merely an up-to-date restatement of the Rolls-Royce philosophy, of the way that this august and dignified concern had always built its cars, and it was confirmation that here was one car, at least, which would continue to be constructed to prewar standards of excellence. No-one, least of all the workforce or the management, doubted that the cars would be built as well at Crewe as they always had been at Derby — assuming, this is, that Robotham's prognostications about the lack of coachbuilding craftsmen had not been over-pessimistic.

Although the war was won, in Europe, in May 1945, and Merlin aero-engine construction had already been running down at Crewe, it was some months before private-car building facilities could be installed, and construction of the first chassis, in any numbers, did not begin before the end of 1945. It was always intended, of course, that Mk VI Bentley and Rolls-Royce Silver Wraith chassis assembly should proceed together up to the point where the Rolls-Royce chassis was ready to be despatched to the coachbuilder, so to a certain extent the start of Silver Wraith assembly depended on the Bentley's state of readiness, too. In the event, the Silver Wraith made its bow in April 1946 and the Bentley was launched seven weeks later.

In fact, even that launch was a tiny bit premature, for the first prototype (chassis number 34G8, not in the production series) was delivered to Hoopers on February 14, 1946, and only artists' impressions of coachwork style were available by early April. A second prototype chassis (WTA1) went to H.J. Mulliner on May 20, 1946. There was then a considerable delay while styles were settled, priorities discussed and construction completed, and search of the chassis records reveals that the first Silver Wraith for a private (*i.e.* non-Rolls-Royce company) customer, was not delivered until February 4, 1947, the lucky recipient being Mr D.F.S. Henderson, of Houston, in Renfrewshire, Scotland.

[Bentley Mk VI deliveries, while also delayed, had not been held up so much, for the first car was handed over on September 21, 1946, just four months after the model had first been revealed.]

Not only did great coachbuilding specialists like H.J. Mulliner, Park Ward (a Rolls-Royce subsidiary, remember), Hooper and James Young have to get their craftsmen out of the armed forces — a process which took many months in some cases — and re-equip their premises again, but their designers had to catch their breath, look around and come to terms with postwar tastes and conditions.

The coachbuilders mentioned above, along with other illustrious concerns like Gurney Nutting and Freestone & Webb, all had premises in the London area. Even if these had not been damaged by enemy bombing, the businesses had been totally immersed in projects such as the building of wooden De Havilland Mosquito or Hamilcar glider sections, and would need time to be reconverted. There was also the well-publicized shortage of everything — from seasoned wood to sheet steel, from heating fuel to the availability of labour — and, as all were soon to find out, enough wealthy customers. In 1945 there had been a social and political upheaval, one consequence of which was that taxation of high incomes had become very fierce indeed, so it was something of a miracle that *anyone* could now afford to buy a bespoke car.

All of which is to forget that wars breed inflation, lots of it. I need only mention that a coachbuilt 1939 Wraith had cost about £1,600, with no extra taxes to be paid, whereas a 1947 Silver Wraith cost about £3,400 basic (depending on the choice of body style), or no less than £4,350 when the new-fangled and hated Purchase Tax had been paid. In just eight years, the price had increased by 270%!

But the miracle came to pass, after all — a seven-year period without new cars ensured that — and a steady queue of customers soon developed to buy the Silver Wraith. It mattered not that it was the only new type of Rolls-Royce available, for it was a very fine chassis, and coachwork styles were likely to be as elegant as ever. Right from the start, there was a choice of approved body styles from Rolls-Royce — a sports saloon and limousine from Park Ward, a sedanca de ville from H.J. Mulliner and a touring limousine from Hooper — and more would follow

In this instance, H.J. Mulliner squeezed as much passenger space as possible out of the Silver Wraith chassis, for seven-seater accommodation, and as a result the rear is rather high and upright.

25

The Hooper coachbuilding factory at Acton, in 1957, showing a pleasing line-up of Rolls-Royce, Bentley and Daimler cars, all in for attention. Happy days!

Occasionally, a Silver Wraith would be clothed by a European coachbuilder. This was a 1947 Franay drophead coupe.

This truly horrid Silver Wraith at the Geneva motor show of 1949 had a body by Poberejsky. Sir Henry Royce would have been appalled.

Hooper were inspired (or persuaded) to produce this amazingly ugly Silver Wraith for the extrovert millionaire Nubar Gulbenkian. I can only hope it has not survived.

in the future.

In every case, the 1946-47 styles remained faithful to enormous free-standing headlamps, mounted high up at each side of the proud and unmistakable radiator grille, though one immediate sign of postwar modernization — 'streamlining' even — was that separate running-boards were hidden away, only becoming obvious when outswept doors were opened. Compared with prewar, and to match the disappearance of the running-boards, the rear-end width of the shells was increased, such that the rear wings themselves became much less prominent.

It was interesting to note, too, that the radiator of the Silver Wraith was several inches further forward on the chassis frame than it had been on that of the Wraith (well ahead of the inner pivots of the front suspension, rather than parallel with them), the engine, bulkhead, pedals and driving position had all been moved forward to suit, and there was at least as much room inside a coachbuilt shell as ever before, even though the postwar car's wheelbase was 9 inches less than before. The driver sat almost exactly in the middle of the wheelbase, the rear seat was well ahead of the line of the rear axle, and the standard distance from the pedals of the leading edge of the rear seat was 67 inches. It was no wonder that no-one was complaining.

One of the very last longer-wheelbase Silver Wraith chassis of 1958 was given this interesting, if not totally graceful, all-weather body style by Hooper. The Perspex roof could be removed, and a conventional drophead coupe top erected instead.

The cognoscenti could recognize a particular coachbuilder's 'signature' by the lines of the bodyshell, particularly around the tail, though naturally all were constrained to use the same radiator shell and bulkhead/scuttle profile, for these were supplied by Rolls-Royce as part of the rolling chassis. Hooper, of course, had developed and were still refining their semi-razor-edge style seen before the war (and aped, none too successfully, by Standard-Triumph with the 1800 saloon of 1946), H.J. Mulliner had a quite distinctive rear-quarter layout which would be retained for some years, and the Park Ward saloons were beginning to look almost rakish. In the main, bodyshells were still traditional, composite structures, where seasoned wood formed the skeleton and steel or aluminium sheet was lovingly hand-crafted to cover this, though Park Ward were still in the van of all-metal construction, and their rivals, tentatively, but inevitably, would eventually follow their lead.

At first, every Silver Wraith built had right-hand drive, though a good proportion of those early cars were destined for an overseas customer. 'Export or Die' was the British Government's exhortation, and because sheet steel supplies were linked to a company's export performance, the coachbuilders were happy to comply. Although the first left-hand-drive Mk VI Bentley was delivered in March 1949, the first such Silver Wraith chassis was not despatched until December of the same year — actually going to France for an unknown bodyshell to be added by mid-1950.

[This chassis, in fact, had been built in the summer of 1948, and shown at the Earls Court exhibition in October of that year, but then, haste has never been one of the failings of the great Rolls-Royce concern!]

All of the 'separate-chassis' cars covered in these two books, incidentally, carry the letter 'L' (for left-hand steering) as a prefix to their conventional chassis number. The original French-bound Silver Wraith chassis, therefore, was LWAB63. Once available, of course, the left-hand-drive option became very popular, especially for cars sold to the United States, and the proportion of left-hand-drive cars soon built up rapidly. I ought to make the point that the first left-hand-drive Rolls-Royce (as opposed to Bentley) was the original Silver Dawn, built from April 1949, whose development as an export-only car

28

The James Young line-up of 1951, with a Silver Wraith in the foreground and coachbuilt Bentley Mk VIs behind it.

No matter what the bulk, a James Young style was invariably well-proportioned, like this sedanca de ville body on the Silver Wraith chassis.

Silver Wraith by James Young, appropriately enough outside their own Bromley showrooms.

made left-hand steering essential.

Once production of the Silver Wraith was 'on stream', and the favoured coachbuilders had a series of 'standard' styles to offer their demanding customers, it seemed to take five to six months between delivery of the chassis to the coachbuilder and delivery of the finished car to the customer. The customers, it seems, were not unhappy at this seemingly leisurely process, as they knew that a Rolls-Royce was not likely to be rendered obsolete overnight, that styles were in any case only in a state of gentle evolution, and that the delays were the same for everyone else!

The Silver Wraith, in fact, was to remain on sale for 13 years (although the last rolling chassis was delivered to H.J. Mulliner a full year before the model was displaced by the Phantom V), and it went through a series of important mechanical improvements in that time, all being phased in to suit the more 'mass-production' requirements of the Bentley and Rolls-Royce 'standard-steel' models. The car, in fact, spanned the entire life of the overhead-inlet-side-exhaust-valve series of engines, for when the old six-cylinder was dropped in 1959, so was the Silver Wraith itself.

Briefly, the major mechanical changes applied to the Silver Wraith were that an enlarged (4,566cc) engine was standardized in 1951, a lengthened wheelbase was phased in within weeks of this, and automatic transmission became optional in mid-1952.

The registration number suggests factory ownership (it is from Cheshire), while this Silver Wraith is equipped with a Park Ward limousine body style dating from the late 1950s.

The final engine stretch, to 4,887cc, came in 1954, and an update to twin SU carburettors (Silver Cloud/S-Series type) was made in 1956.

For the 'standard-steel' saloons, most of these changes had been to improve the cars' performance, and keep them abreast of current trends. In the case of the Silver Wraith, there was little pressure from customers to make faster cars, but there always seemed to be a tendency for the overall weight of the bodies to increase. For that reason alone, therefore, it was perhaps a

blessing that the peak power output increased from something like 122bhp in 1946 to nearly 180bhp in 1959.

Those people shopping around for a Silver Wraith today will want to be able to pinpoint certain important development 'junctions' and these are that the wheelbase was increased by 6 inches (and the rear track by 4 inches at the same time) from the start of the ALW chassis series. First complete car deliveries of long-wheelbase models came early in 1952, and all long-wheelbase models carry a chassis number with the letters LW

This Freestone & Webb Silver Wraith had neat door pockets, and even the gear lever knob matched the door and seat trim colours . . .

. . . while the division glass was retractable and there was a cocktail cabinet between the fold-down picnic tables.

This 1957 Park Ward Silver Wraith limousine even provided space for a small TV set in the division structure.

A Park Ward-bodied Silver Wraith of 1957 in which a Minifon wire (not tape) recorder was housed in a wide centre armrest.

Seen at an RREC Duxford gathering in 1984 was this splendid black-and-cream Hooper-bodied Silver Wraith. That boot must be cavernous.

second and third in the identification sequence. Incidentally, there was an overlap of about one year with the last of the shorter-wheelbase Silver Wraith chassis.

Just a few of the final shorter-wheelbase Silver Wraiths had manual transmission, along with some longer-wheelbase examples, but the vast majority of these cars had the automatic transmission. It was to make sure that no performance was lost in the fluid coupling of the transmission that the engine's compression ratio was raised to 6.75:1 at around the same time. All of the longer-wheelbase cars, incidentally, seem to have been fitted with 16-inch road wheels.

The striking feature of the Silver Wraith, of course, was not its chassis, but the style and quality of its coachwork. In this case, and with other coachbuilt models covered in this volume, I have tended to let the illustrations tell their own story. The vast majority of Silver Wraith styles, naturally, were big, spacious,

Park Ward's six-light saloon bodywork was a popular style for the Silver Wraith chassis in the early 1950s. This immaculately preserved car was also on view at Duxford in 1984.

35

dignified and unmistakably Rolls-Royce, especially as that famous radiator style was retained. Although the standard Mk VI Bentley always featured semi-recessed headlamps, very few Silver Wraith styles used this detail until the early 1950s. By the the mid-1950s, however, styles were at least matching those of the latest 'standard-steel'Rolls-Royce, the Silver Cloud, and a final Silver Wraith style was very similar to that of the early Phantom V, which was to follow.

Occasionally, taste took a back seat and the results were disappointing, even horrendous at times. One style by Hooper was so bad that it had to be the result of a nightmare, or an insistent order from a customer, while there was a really nasty Geneva motor show monstrosity by a foreign coachbuilder. The British stylists, in general, felt their way very carefully towards modern lines, the result being that the early slab-sided creations were too plain, and the detail rather clumsy.

In general, however, most Silver Wraiths were very desirable-looking cars indeed, especially those long and rakish sports saloons built by companies like Hooper, or Freestone & Webb. The majority, as one might expect, were large and capacious limousines, almost always with a division and occasional seats in the rear compartment, some facing forward, some sideways. As the years passed by, the rear compartments tended to be equipped with ever more 'personal' equipment; radios were commonplace, then tape recorders were added, black-and-white TV receivers at times, personal controls for the ventilation system, and the inevitable drinks compartment and fold-down tables. The working businessman, too, might have an intercom to his chauffeur, reading lights to allow him to work while being whisked from home, dictaphones and pull-out surfaces on which to make notes. A Silver Wraith was, or could be, all things to all (wealthy) men.

Although the Silver Wraith sold well (1,144 cars with the original wheelbase, 639 with the longer wheelbase, making 1,783 cars in all), it was never built at an enormous rate. The chassis was built at Crewe for 12 years, and this equates to an average production rate of less than 150 cars a year, or about three cars a week. [By comparison, a total of 490 Wraiths were built in little more than a year, between autumn 1938 and the run-down of chassis production at Derby after the outbreak of war in September 1939.]

Silver Wraith sales ran down rapidly once the 'standard-steel' Silver Cloud had been launched in 1955, and less than 200 cars were built in the last three years it was on the market. The last but one chassis (LHLW51) left Crewe for Hoopers on September 24, 1958, and the last of all (LHLW52) went to H.J. Mulliner on October 10, 1958. However, the last *delivery*, from Hoopers, was made to the Ghanaian Embassy in Bonn, on August 15, 1959, just before the Silver Wraith became obsolete and was replaced by the Phantom V.

When the Silver Wraith was joined in 1950 by the Phantom IV — the 'Royal Rolls-Royce', which I describe in the next chapter — it lost its 'largest postwar Rolls-Royce' title, but that car, in any case, would be eclipsed by the gargantuan Phantom V. It is also worth pointing out, too, that the *basic* Silver Wraith chassis design had been rendered obsolescent from April 1955, when the Silver Dawn/R-Type model was replaced by the Silver Cloud/S-Series cars.

The Silver Wraith, however, had a long and distinguished career and holds one record, never likely to be broken. More Silver Wraiths were built than any other type of postwar coachbuilt-bodied Rolls-Royce.

CHAPTER 3

Rolls-Royce Phantom IV

The only straight-eight from Rolls-Royce

The most outstanding feature of the Phantom IV, revealed in 1950, was not that it was to be so exclusive (the sales policy was simple — examples would only be supplied to Royalty and Heads of State), but that it was the first eight-cylinder production car which Rolls-Royce had ever built. In this regard, I choose to ignore the curious V8 'Legalimit/Invisible Engine' machines of 1905-06, which never truly went into production.

There were several reasons why Rolls-Royce should have chosen to use an eight-cylinder engine well before this, but several good technical reasons why they should not. What is interesting is that, in the 1920s and 1930s, Sir Henry Royce and his team chose to ignore the vogue for straight-eights which swept through Europe and the United States at that time. It is said that they were not then convinced that such an engine's block and crankshaft could be made rigid enough to satisfy Royce's very high standards, and that in any case they were content with the smoothness, sophistication and general behaviour of their own six-cylinder engines. Certainly when Royce came to sketch out a new unit to replace the old Phantom I/Phantom II engine, he chose to leapfrog the eight-cylinder solution altogether and went for a V12 engine for the Phantom III.

In Volume 1 of this Rolls-Royce/Bentley book, and in previous chapters of this volume, I have explained that Rolls-Royce proposed to develop a new, wide, but rationalized range of engines and chassis towards the end of the 1930s, had development examples of all types running around during the Second World War, and at one time proposed to put all of them on sale immediately after the war. Three distinctly different eight-cylinder-engined prototypes were being developed during the war — a vast seven-seater Rolls-Royce limousine nicknamed 'Big Bertha', a shorter-wheelbase Rolls-Royce, still with a division, which was often used by E.W. Hives, and a Bentley Mk V-based sports saloon called 'Scalded Cat'.

Purely on economic considerations, however, Rolls-Royce decided to concentrate their postwar resources on the new i.o.e. six-cylinder engine at first. Everything they learned from those units was applied to the related four-cylinder and straight-eight engines, though for the time being these did not find a home. Quite soon, in fact, the idea of producing a four-cylinder-engined Rolls-Royce was abandoned, and the engine eventually found a home in the FV1800 four-wheel-drive vehicle intended by the British Army to replace the ubiquitous Jeep.

Development cars fitted with the eight-cylinder engine continued to be used at Crewe, and occasionally, favoured personalities were allowed to sample them. In particular, Rolls-Royce allowed 'Scalded Cat' to be tested on several private occasions, notably by H.R.H. the Duke of Edinburgh. It is only fair, however, to confirm that 'Scalded Cat' was not only much faster than any previous Rolls-Royce or Bentley, but it also had singularly precarious handling; in spite of pleas from enthusiasts with bottomless pockets for cars to be put on sale, the company was never convinced.

In the meantime, and in spite of the austerity-conscious atmosphere of the late 1940s, the company found a small, but definite demand for a car even more luxurious, spacious and stately than the existing Silver Wraith. The magnificent (if not very reliable) Phantom III of 1935-39 had been one such car, but

For the very limited-production Phantom IV cars, Rolls-Royce chose to use the eight-cylinder B80 engine of 5.67 litres, which was clearly a derivative of the more usual six-cylinder B60.

after the technical upheaval of the late 1930s/early 1940s, there seemed to be no immediate place for a successor.

At this point, apparently, the Duke of Edinburgh tried 'Scalded Cat' and suggested that a limousine with that engine should be produced. It would be stretching a point to suggest that Rolls-Royce decided, there and then, to produce the Phantom IV, but the possibility of providing a car to the heir to the British throne, Princess Elizabeth, must have been attractive. There had been Rolls-Royce sales to members of the British Royal Family in the past, but throughout the century the Sovereign had always used Daimlers as official cars; the possibility of changing this tradition must have been attractive, to say the least!

This, then, was certainly one inspiration behind the Phantom IV, which was announced in July 1950 just as the first example, complete with H.J. Mulliner limousine bodyshell, was being delivered to H.R.H. Princess Elizabeth. Superficially it looked like any other contemporary Mulliner-bodied Rolls-Royce, but mechanically it was quite different, for not only did it have the big eight-cylinder engine, but its wheelbase had been stretched to no less than 12ft 1in. [There must have been something significant about this dimension, for it cropped up again on the

Massive but dignified three-quarter rear view of 4AF2, the H.J. Mulliner-bodied Phantom IV delivered to H.R.H. Princess Elizabeth in 1950. This car is still in use by the Royal Household in the mid-1980s.

Phantom V and VI models, even though these cars were not even closely related to the Phantom IV!]

The story of the Phantom IV, therefore, must surely begin with the engine itself, if only because it was such a landmark in Rolls-Royce private car history. In years to come, for sure, a whole variety of military and commercial vehicles would also be equipped with this type of engine (I vividly recall a spirited demonstration in a Rolls-Royce-powered Alvis Stalwart . . .), but it was, and remains, the only straight-eight-powered Rolls-Royce car ever to be put on sale.

In mid-1938, the design of a new family of engines had got under way, which were radically different from previous Rolls-Royce units, not only because they had overhead inlet and side exhaust valves, but also because the cylinder block and crankcase were to be cast in unit for the first time. Coded B40, B60 and B80, these engines shared common bore and stroke dimensions, pistons, connecting rods and valve gear. Accordingly, the B80 straight-eight had a swept volume of 5,675cc, at a time when the 'standard' B60 size was still 4,257cc. [The mind boggles at the implications of a straight-eight using

the later B60 (4,887cc) engine's cylinder bore — for its capacity would have been no less than 6,516cc!]

Details of the straight-eight engine had already been revealed in April 1948, when it was seen to have an aluminium cylinder head, a downdraught dual-choke Stromberg carburettor and a nine-bearing crankshaft. It was, of course, a lengthy unit, and a bulky one, which explains why the fully-equipped weight was 1,000lb, compared with 820lb for the six-cylinder B60, and this may partly explain why the handling of 'Scalded Cat' was somewhat suspect!

Because this range of units announced in 1948 was for 'commercial', rather than private car use, Rolls-Royce were happy to announce peak power and torque figures. The B60 (Silver Wraith-type) six-cylinder engine was quoted at 126bhp at 3,750rpm and 227lb/ft torque at 1,800rpm, while the impressive eight-cylinder B80 was quoted at 162bhp at 3,750rpm and 282lb/ft at 1,750rpm. Even when it came to be installed in the Phantom IV, complete with air cleaners and comprehensive silencing, it was probably the most powerful and refined car engine in the UK.

Two views of the facia and driving controls of the Phantom IV model, the rarest of all postwar Rolls-Royce models. This, in fact, was the car supplied to H.R.H. Princess Elizabeth in 1950 — note the switch for the Police Light to the far left of the instrument panel. There are detail similarities (and perhaps some common components) to the Silver Dawn of the period.

The other Phantom IV in the Royal Household, equipped with a Hooper landaulette body, was delivered to H.M. The Queen early in her reign. Like the original car, 4BP5 is still in use.

The dictator of Spain, Generalissimo Franco, bought no fewer than three Phantom IVs, this example being a seven-seater limousine by H.J. Mulliner, almost identical in looks to that supplied to H.R.H. Princess Elizabeth, but fitted out with full armour-plating!

Because the B80 was such a massive engine, and there was a requirement for an extremely roomy limousine body style, the new car needed its really long wheelbase of 12ft 1in. Although its chassis frame was of the same general design and layout as that of the current Mk VI Bentley/Rolls-Royce Silver Dawn (10ft 0in) and the Silver Wraith (10ft 7in), different channel-section side-members and a different cruciform X-member had to be provided. When the centre of the cruciform is studied, this becomes obvious, for the profile is quite unique, and many more rivets than usual are employed in the fixings.

Even so, mainly standard components from the Silver Wraith were used in the front and rear suspensions, steering, transmission, rear axle, mechanically-operated servo and drum braking installation. In the case of the Phantom IV, however, there was a 23 Imperial gallon fuel tank, with two filler necks (one in each rear wing). The road wheels were of a new design, being fixed to the brake drums by no fewer than 10 studs each and 7.00-17in tyres were specified.

The very first production car (30GVII and 33GVII, both used by Hives, had effectively been the prototypes) was delivered to Princess Elizabeth on July 6, 1950, though the rolling chassis had been sent to H.J. Mulliner as early as July 1949. The bodyshell, as one might expect, was a stately, dignified and supremely elegant piece of sculpture, recognizably the same as other shells coming from the Chiswick premises at the time. Naturally it had a division, and the rear doors were hinged at the rear so that the occupants could descend gracefully on ceremonial occasions. Interesting features in this shell included detachable panels, which could be fixed inside the rear quarter-windows to enhance rear seat privacy (in fact I have never seen pictures with these in place), rear seats which could be wound forward so that the occupants could be seen more easily, and a transparent panel above the rear seats which could be obscured with a motor-driven shutter.

The fact that an H.J. Mulliner style had been chosen was a real break from Royal tradition, for previous official Daimlers had usually been bodied by Hooper. H.J. Mulliner, however, had made a truly elegant job of what was (and still is!) a very large car indeed. Not only was it nearly 19ft long, but it stood 6ft 2in high and was 6ft 5in wide. Even so, there was not enough space for the

The standard H.J. Mulliner body style for the Phantom IV limousine, a picture taken inside the Mulliner workshops. Note the great length (12ft 1in) of the car's wheelbase.

If a proud Phantom IV owner or chauffeur ever needed to open the bonnet, he would have been confronted with this magnificent and lengthy eight-cylinder power unit. All the electrical fittings on the bulkhead are by Joseph Lucas, of course.

twin spare wheels to be carried internally, so they were mounted under covers, tucked into the front wings, behind and rather higher than the front wheels.

At no time was a Phantom IV ever subjected to the indignity of a magazine road test, but we can nevertheless make a fair guess at the performance of such a car. It was even larger (higher and wider) than the contemporary Silver Wraith, and somewhat heavier, so most of the extra engine power and torque would be needed even to maintain the *status quo*. It seems reasonable, though, to estimate a top speed, if required, of about 100mph, though hard driving would almost certainly have reduced the fuel consumption to worse than 10mpg!

History does not record if Princess Elizabeth or the Duke of Edinburgh ever drove this car, but if so they would no doubt have been disappointed by the driving position, for the backrest was rather upright, there was no fore-and-aft adjustment, rather restricted space and, of course, no power assistance to the steering. Even today, nearly 35 years after it was built, this unregistered car is still retained by the Royal Household, along with another Phantom IV (see below) and the three high-roofed 'Canberra' Phantom Vs and VIs. Need I say that it is still in immaculate, as-new, condition?

H.R.H. Princess Elizabeth's Phantom IV rear compartment, showing one occasional seat folded up for use, and the radio set controls in the central armrest.

Because so very few Phantom IVs were ever built — 18 in less than six years — and because each was so special in one way or another, I have assembled brief details of each car, its body style, and its original illustrious owner:

Chassis No	Body style	Original owner
4AF2	H.J. Mulliner limousine (later converted to automatic transmission)	H.R.H. Princess Elizabeth (now H.M. The Queen)
4AF4	Open delivery wagon!	Rolls-Royce Ltd
4AF6	H.J. Mulliner drophead coupe	The Shah of Iran
4AF8	H.J. Mulliner saloon	The Ruler of Kuwait
4AF10	Hooper limousine	The Duke of Gloucester
4AF12	Hooper limousine (later became automatic transmission)	The Duchess of Kent
4AF14	H.J. Mulliner limousine	General Franco of Spain
4AF16	H.J. Mulliner limousine	General Franco of Spain
4AF18	H.J. Mulliner cabriolet	General Franco of Spain
4AF20	Hooper sedanca de ville	The Aga Khan
4AF22	Franay (of France)	Prince Talal al Saoud Ryal of Saudi Arabia
4BP1	Hooper limousine	King Feisal of Iraq
4BP3	Hooper limousine	The Prince Regent of Iraq
4BP5	Hooper Landaulette (with automatic transmission)	H.M. The Queen
4BP7	H.J. Mulliner limousine (with automatic transmission)	H.R.H. Princess Margaret
4CS2	H.J. Mulliner saloon	The Ruler of Kuwait
4CS4	H.J. Mulliner saloon	The Ruler of Kuwait
4CS6	Hooper limousine	The Shah of Iran

Each and every example of the Phantom IV, of course, would have its own story to tell — if only because of its original destination. It is worth noting that no less than eight of the 18

This great Phantom IV drophead coupe, with coachwork by H.J. Mulliner, was only a four-seater, and it went to the Shah of Iran in 1951. Pity about the headlamp style . . .

originally went to Middle Eastern countries, while only six (of which one was retained by Rolls-Royce Ltd) stayed in this country at first. The Spanish military dictator, General Franco, obviously loved the Phantom IV, for he not only took delivery of three examples, but they all left for Spain within weeks of each other in 1952. The order date of those cars, incidentally, is still known — October 18, 1948 — which indicates how long it was between Rolls-Royce's decision to start building strictly limited numbers of these cars, and their actual availability.

Clearly, such a project could have been no more than an indulgence for the company, and I am sure that each chassis frame was hand-built by John Thompson Pressings for the purpose. Incidentally, before any collector gets enthusiastic over the idea of discovering the Phantom IV once owned by Rolls-Royce themselves, I think I should say that it was originally bodied as a delivery wagon (!) and that it was broken up in 1963 . . .

The first of these cars was delivered in 1940 and the last rolling chassis (for the Shah of Iran) was completed in December 1955, though the complete car was not ready for despatch until November 1956. When the Phantom IV was originally put on sale, the Rolls-Royce/GM automatic transmission was not ready for use, and in the end only two cars — 4BP5 for H.M. The Queen and 4BP7 for H.R.H. Princess Margaret — were equipped with automatic transmission from new. Two other cars — 4AF2 (H.M. The Queen's original car) and 4AF12 (the Duchess of Kent) — were converted from manual to automatic transmission during 1954.

Most of the Phantom IVs built are still in existence, and are naturally highly prized if they have been sold into private hands. I understand, however, that in the 1950s one of the conditions of sale imposed by Rolls-Royce was that the cars should not be sold by their illustrious owners, but should be returned to the factory.

Demand for these intriguing Phantom IVs was always tiny, and I suspect that Rolls-Royce were happy to phase it out when the Bentley Mk VI/R-Type/Silver Dawn model was replaced by the Silver Cloud/S-Series in 1955, even though the Silver Wraith (whose chassis engineering was closely related to that of the Phantom IV) continued for a while. The Phantom V, which followed in 1959, was not related in any mechanical respect.

45

This is one of three Phantom IVs delivered to Generalissimo Franco of Spain, in 1952, with drophead coupe coachwork by H.J. Mulliner.

CHAPTER 4

Rolls-Royce Phantom V and VI

A whole generation of dignity

In all the fuss that went into celebrating the 25 years of BMC/BL Mini production in the autumn of 1984, few people remembered that the Rolls-Royce Phantom V/Phantom VI chassis, introduced at the same time, had also reached that milestone. Even though its annual production had fallen right away — to less than 10 cars a year at times — the Phantom VI, like the Mini, was still part of the contemporary motoring scene.

Devoted Rolls-Royce watchers must have realized that the popular Silver Wraith was living on borrowed time once the Silver Dawn/R-Type chassis was displaced by the Silver Cloud/S-Series layout in 1955, so it was inevitable that a new model would have to take its place. It was a surprise to everyone except Rolls-Royce, no doubt, that this change was delayed for more than four years.

The change, when it came in the autumn of 1959, was neatly arranged to coincide with the arrival of the new light-alloy V8 engine to take over from the long-running straight 'six'. None of this, in fairness, was much of a surprise to the motoring media, who had known of the development of the new V8 engine for some years. The surprise, really, was in the choice of name for the new car; to replace the Silver Wraith, perhaps it would have been reasonable to expect a new 'Silver . . .', but instead, Rolls-Royce chose to call the new car the Phantom V, even though it had no direct links with the very rare straight-eight Phantom IV, or with any of the prewar Phantoms.

It is basically correct, but not in detail, to say that the Phantom V had the same chassis design as that of the current Silver Cloud/S-Series saloons. As with the thinking behind the original 'rationalized' cars of the 1940s, Harry Grylls' team had set out in 1950 to provide a new standard 'foundation' for a whole range of cars, but to allow for different wheelbase lengths at the same time.

The chassis-frame of the new Phantom V, therefore, was closely related to that of the Silver Cloud II (complete with its light-alloy V8 engine and the Hydramatic automatic transmission), though the wheelbase, at 12ft 1in, was 22 inches longer than that of the 'standard-steel' cars, while its wheel tracks, especially at the rear, were also wider; front wishbones were an inch longer at each side, while the rear axle had 2-inch longer tubes at each side. The general layout, which included a strong cruciform 'X'-member, box-section main members and the unmistakable Rolls-Royce attention to detail, were all the same, and Silver Cloud II features, such as power-assisted steering, 11.25×3in drum brakes with the famous transmission-driven mechanical servo, and ride stiffness control of the rear dampers, were all present.

Features special to the Phantom V chassis, however, included the use of a fatter (8.90in) tyre section on the same 15in road wheels, and the lack of a rear suspension 'Z'-bar. The latter had gone in the interests of improved refinement, rather than for any good roadholding or related technical reasons. It was thought that a Phantom V, nearly 20 feet long and weighing well over 5,000lb at the kerb side, was not likely to be driven to its limits very often.

I hope I need say very little about the $6\frac{1}{4}$-litre V8 engine at this stage, not only because it has become an extremely well-known design and has been in use at Rolls-Royce for more than 25 years, but because its design and development is more fully covered in

When Rolls-Royce were developing the chassis of the Phantom V, they used this temporary bodyshell, in which a down-at-heel Bentley radiator shell figured strongly.

Osmond Rivers, once Hopper's noted chief body designer, produced this individual shape for a Phantom V bodied by Henri Chapron of Paris.

The 12ft 1in-wheelbase Phanton V rolling chassis, ready to leave Crewe for coachwork to be added at Park Ward or James Young, in left-hand-drive form. Note that only the inner bulkhead panel was supplied by the factory. The trunking around the front wheel is all connected with the heating and ventilation system.

Volume 1, which deals with the 'standard-steel' cars. It is enough to say that it was — and is — a marvellously refined, if quite complex unit, developed up to the highest Rolls-Royce standards of design and tradition, that it produced steam-engine-like torque from very low speeds, and was as silent and flexible as a Rolls-Royce engine should be.

The automatic transmission was the RR/GM unit which had been standardized on contemporary Rolls-Royce and Bentley models for some time, which is to say that there was a fluid coupling, but no torque converter, and four forward speeds. The control was on the steering column, as usual. Because of the added weight and bulk of the Phantom V compared with the obsolete Silver Wraith, also because many cars could be expected to spend a lot of their time drifting slowly through crowded city streets or in ceremonial processions, the final drive for the new car was given a 3.89:1 ratio, compared with 3.08:1 for the Silver Cloud II saloon. An even lower (higher numerically) ratio had been available for the Silver Wraith from 1955.

For the customers, however, the attraction of the Phantom V was in the intriguing combination of tradition and novelty — the latter encompassing the engine and the new chassis design, the former involving the general range of body styles, the equipment, the accommodation — and the dimensions! No doubt it was done to encourage the coachbuilders merely to evolve existing limited-production body styles, but the Phantom V's wheelbase of 12ft 1in was the same as that of the obsolete Phantom IV, while the rear wheel track was 5ft 4in, the same as that of the last Silver Wraith, and only marginally wider than that of the Phantom IV.

Described very basically, if not delicately, the Phantom V was an enormous car by any standards, so *The Autocar* was quite right to headline its technical description: 'Largest Rolls-Royce ever built.' Covering this massive chassis was a choice of seven-passenger limousines from Park Ward or James Young, or a touring limousine from James Young. The 'standard' design, chosen by a large proportion of the clientele, was the spacious but

Considering the sheer size of the Phantom V chassis, this James Young sedanca de ville body style was astonishingly successful. JB 1 was the famous Jack Barclay personalized number — James Young being owned by that group. The two-headlamp nose dates this as a pre-1963 car . . .

graceful Park Ward style, which was no less than 19ft 10in long and 6ft 7in wide; not even the typical prewar Phantom III (17ft 9in), or eight-cylinder Phantom IV (18ft 11in on the very first example), could match that. Nor could any of the monstrous Cadillacs or Lincolns from the United States beat it, either.

Because of its size, the Phantom V was inescapably a very heavy car, and even the first examples were listed at about 5,600lb/2,540kg. In later years, as increasingly more complex equipment was specified, the weight crept inexorably up towards 6,000lb/2,721kg, ensuring that the car was not only the largest, but also the heaviest, in the world.

As usual, Rolls-Royce proposed to build these cars at Crewe, up to the complete rolling chassis stage, then to deliver them to approved coachbuilders for bodies to be added. In general, they tried to ensure that the chassis were only clothed by Park Ward

(their own subsidiary), or James Young (which was a member of the Jack Barclay Group — a noted Rolls-Royce distributor — and built graceful bodies at Bromley, in Kent).

Surprisingly, there were to be very few H.J. Mulliner-styled cars at first, even though the Chiswick-based concern had been taken over by Rolls-Royce in the summer of 1959. This was not because H.J. Mulliner was out of favour with Crewe, but because the company was thought to have quite enough on its plate with the development of a Silver Cloud/S-Series drophead coupe (almost a two-door lookalike of the saloon in terms of wing lines and general profile) and with the continuing production of Bentley Continentals.

In each and every case, of course, the proportions of a Phantom V limousine, with or without a division, were defined by the very long wheelbase, wide tracks and the need for a lot of

... but the very last was built in 1967, by which time the four-headlamp nose had been adopted and the outline of the rear quarter-windows had been slightly — and successfully — modified.

spacious accommodation, but in general the cars produced were all very well-balanced, and some (like the Park Ward style, which is still with us in the mid-1980s) had lines which were unmistakably related to those of the Silver Cloud II. Just for the record, I note that the Phantom V was launched at the end of September 1959, and that when the Earls Court motor show opened its doors on October 21, Phantom V styles were on display on the Hooper, H.J. Mulliner, Park Ward and James Young stands. Since I now know that only two cars were actually *delivered* in 1959 (both being James Young models), it seems likely that some of those Earls Court exhibits were mechanically incomplete!

Let us remember, too, that prices had risen yet again, and put the Phantom V into its accepted place in the British motoring scene. When it went on sale, in October 1959, the Phantom V cost a total of £8,905 with the Park Ward limousine shell, £9,394 with the rival James Young offering, and £9,110 if the James Young touring limousine body was chosen instead. Compare this price level with the £5,802 for a Bentley S2 Continental, and a mere £4,340 for a 4½-litre Daimler DK400B

limousine, and you can immediately see why the Phantom V was likely to occupy a very small, but exclusive, place in the market. It was, in short, the most costly car sold in Great Britain up to that moment.

To put the Phantom V into true perspective, one had to compare it with more mundane machinery, and in a fascinating and unique road test published in 1962, *The Motor* tried a Park Ward-bodied limousine (registered 98 PMA, a Cheshire number) and reminded its readers that: 'To use a familiar yardstick, a Mini-Minor saloon stands 3½ inches above the Rolls-Royce radiator emblem, and two of these cars end to end would be 2½ inches longer than the Park Ward limousine.' Which, if nothing else, emphasized how lofty the patrician radiator and 'Flying Lady' still was — and what a small car the Mini was, as well.

Some of the dimensions defining the sheer size of the bodyshell (which stayed in production, basically unchanged, for the next 25 years, of course) are instructive, including the 8ft 7.7in from the instrument panel to the top of the rear seat, the 5ft 3in dimension across the bench rear seat, and the rather

51

The 1963 four-headlamp James Young Phantom V touring limousine had remarkably similar lines to . . .

. . . those of the long-wheelbase Silver Cloud III of the same year. Most of the changes are grouped around the rear — note the difference in the rear passenger door and the quarter-panels.

cramped nature of the non-adjustable driver's seat. The Park Ward limousine had a permanently fixed division, and was definitely only a chauffeur-driven car, and that chauffeur was meant to sit upright and suffer in silence.

Since all Phantom IIIs of 1936-39 had carried chassis identification starting with the number '3' and the Phantom IVs had used numbers starting with '4', it was only reasonable that the Phantom Vs should be identified by chassis numbers beginning with '5'. Where the car was to have left-hand drive, the 'L' suffix followed this number, and the normal sequence followed that.

Because there had been a considerable lull at Crewe after the last of the Silver Wraiths had left the factory in October 1958, the coachbuilders were ready to tackle a new car as soon as it was obtainable. Well in advance of the production chassis being available, all the major companies had been provided with important dimensions and had produced styling renderings and even partly-built shells by the summer of 1959. The first Phantom V rolling chassis, complete with its V8 engine, automatic transmission and power-assisted steering, was ready to roll several weeks before the equivalent Silver Cloud IIs and Bentley S2s were finished off, and three cars (5LAS2, 5LAS3 and 5AS5) all left for their coachbuilders on July 22, 1959, before the holiday shutdown at Crewe. James Young of Bromley were clearly more advanced than Park Ward, H.J. Mulliner or Hooper (all of whom had plans for the Phantom V), for they delivered 5LAS1, a touring limousine, to the docks for export to New York on September 28, and 5AS17, a seven-seat limousine, on December 9, 1959, but these were the only two cars to be delivered by the end of the year.

For 1960, the original James Young Phantom V seven-passenger limousine had two headlamps, and sidelamps on the peak of the front wings, but . . .

... by the mid-1960s the same shell had been modified to accept a four-headlamp nose, with different side/turn indicator lamps, like this white example delivered to an Indian princess, in which the interior was finished in pure silk.

In the next three years, a total of 239 Phantom Vs were produced, these later being recognized by the fact that they only had two, rather than four headlamps. It is interesting to see how production got away at such a sparkling rate, not only because the Phantom V was such an outstanding product, but because there had been a definite pent-up demand for such a big car, which could not be satisfied once the Silver Wraith had disappeared from the market.

Although H.J. Mulliner and Hooper had both shown examples of their styles on Phantom V chassis at Earls Court in 1959, Hooper almost immediately went out of the coachbuilding business, so their only offering was the black limousine from that show, while their well-known designer Osmond Rivers also shaped a rather angular creation for an American customer, which was actually built by Henri Chapron, of Paris. H.J. Mulliner, taken over by Rolls-Royce even before the Phantom V was launched, built a few touring limousines, but after the amalgamation with Park Ward they dropped that style and found their name added to the 'standard' limousine style from Park Ward.

The James Young styles, even though they were more costly than the Park Ward alternatives, were very successful and (some say) even more attractive. Whereas the Park Ward limousine had wing crown lines sweeping almost straight along the body sides, turning up only slightly over the rear wheelarch behind the rear passenger doors, the James Young style had more swooping lines, a more pronounced rear wheelarch, and a choice of styles, which not only included a touring limousine, which meant that it was suitable for chauffeur or for owner driving, but a very special sedanca-de-ville style in which the roof over the front seats could be retracted and the glass division lowered to give fresh-air motoring for all occupants.

It goes without saying, I am sure, that all the limousines had fold-down occasional seats, picnic tables hinged to the division, and cocktail cabinets in compartments fitted into the division between the tables.

Early on in the life of the Phantom V, too, Park Ward were honoured to supply a pair of special examples to H.M. The Queen, but these (and the Phantom VI which accompanies them) were so special that I have described them in an appendix

The Park Ward (now H.J. Mulliner, Park Ward) limousine body style of the Phantom has now been in production for more than a quarter of a century. Here the original two-headlamp car of 1959 is seen posed outside Osterley Park, in Middlesex.

In spite of the enormous length of 19ft 10in, the Park Ward limousine style on the Phantom V chassis was beautifully proportioned. Original cars had rear-hinged rear doors, this feature being changed in the early 1970s.

If you were wealthy enough (or important enough) to own or use a Park Ward-bodied Phantom V, this would be your view forward over the (partly-lowered) glass division, with cocktail cabinets and picnic tables at the ready. The occasional seats are still folded away.

to this chapter.

Although the Phantom Vs were all very large and heavy, they were also surprisingly rapid machines, especially on good main roads where continuous changes of direction, braking and accelerating were not required. *The Motor's* road test car (a Rolls-Royce demonstrator which had already covered 18,000 miles) was capable of 101mph, and 0-60mph acceleration in 13.8 seconds, though the overall fuel consumption recorded was 11.1mpg (Imperial).

There were, of course, some drawbacks, not least the fact of the ponderous (48ft) turning circle, the perceptible brake servo lag at low speeds, the effective fuel range of a mere 250 miles (about three hours of motoring on fast motorways) and the rather limited roadholding which was quite inescapable from such a large and heavy car. But there was no criticism of the car's appointments, or its comfort: I liked the comment that 'the right-hand passenger [in the rear compartment] has the heater controls and a convenient supply of cigarettes, notepaper and money in leather wallets at his elbow, while his companion can command the radio', for while Rolls-Royce's reputation for attending to detail was legendary, they surely did not supply money in road test cars!

The Phantom V remained in production for nine years, during which several important changes were made to the specification.

Now you see it . . . now you don't. The Phantom V's occasional seats folded neatly away when not required. These, incidentally, are pictures of two different H.J. Mulliner, Park Ward limousines, showing different trim, fittings and ventilation details.

I should point out, too, that although the front-wing refrigeration installation had become standard on the Silver Clouds, the 'in-boot' installation was kept for Phantom Vs for a long period, and it was one of several costly optional extras which many customers specified. In general, because the body styles at H.J. Mulliner, Park Ward and James Young were standardized, it took about three months from the arrival of the chassis before the completed car could be handed over to the customer, or sent to the docks for shipment overseas.

Visually, the only changes made to the cars in nine years were that a landaulette was reluctantly made available, to the right people, and at the right price, the first car being delivered to H.M. The Queen Mother in February 1962, and that from the autumn of 1962 (and the start of the 5VA . . . chassis sequence) the cars were equipped with the Silver Cloud III's high-compression (9:1), extra-powerful engine and the four-headlamp nose with side/indicator lamps recessed into the front of the wings.

The landaulettes, of which there were to be two different types, were very rare indeed. The original type, as typified by H.M. The Queen Mother's car, was provided with a fold-down coupe top above and behind the rear seats only. However, from the autumn of 1965, the company also offered the State Landaulette, in which the folding roof was fixed to the top of the division between the front and rear seats and could uncover much more of the occupants, while at the same time it was provided with an electrically operated rear seat which could be raised by $3\frac{1}{2}$ inches.

All in all, there were only nine Phantom V landaulettes of both types, carrying these chassis numbers: 5CG37, 5VD99*, 5LCG51*, 5LVF29*, 5LVD33*, 5LVF113*, 5LVD41*, 5LVF183*, 5VD83* — only one car remained in the UK, the other eight (their identity marked with an asterisk) all going to overseas customers.

In 1967, the motoring world was sad to see the famous coachbuilding firm of James Young close down, the last of their Phantom Vs being a touring limousine (chassis number 5VF165) delivered at the end of the year. James Young, a subsidiary of the Jack Barclay Group, had been building beautiful bodyshells at Bromley for many years, but their profitability depended on being able to make special coachwork for cars like the Mark VI Bentleys and the Rolls-Royce Silver Clouds. When the Silver Cloud was dropped in 1965, and replaced by the monocoque Silver Shadow, it became clear that this might no longer be possible. Not only would it be much more costly to invest in facilities to build bodies on the basis of the monocoque, but it soon became clear that Rolls-Royce were most reluctant to provide unfinished monocoques for this purpose. James Young, accordingly, produced a mere 50 two-door conversions of the four-door Silver Shadow/T-Series monocoque, then closed their doors.

Although production and deliveries of Phantom Vs progressively slowed during the mid-1960s (the last 182 cars, in the 5VF . . . chassis sequence, occupied Crewe for 26 months, from December 1965 to February 1968), there was never any thought given to dropping the model. Indeed, in the spring of 1968, several months before any official announcement was made, Rolls-Royce started to build Phantom VI models, which were lightly modified Phantom Vs.

Because of the demise of James Young, all Phantom VIs with British coachwork used the same imposing H.J. Mulliner, Park Ward body style (limousine, or *very* occasionally, a landaulette); my researches, by courtesy of Rolls-Royce Motors, have also revealed two Phantom VI chassis (PRH4643 and PRH4705) as being shipped to Italy for special Frua coachwork to be erected. In general, however, it is almost impossible to 'pick' a Phantom VI from a Phantom V.

The differences between the two models were relatively minor — and compared with the change, say, from Phantom IV to Phantom V, they were insignificant. Externally, there were no changes, but inside the big passenger compartment there was a different facia layout for the chauffeur, and there were separate air-conditioning/refrigeration installations for front and rear compartments as standard. The front-seat unit was similar to that used on the current Silver Shadow, installed behind the facia, with swivelling facia-mounted vents, while that for the rear compartment was still mounted in the boot, as had always been the case with the Phantom V. The rear compartment was upholstered in all-wool twill material, though the front seats still had best British leather hide. The price, naturally, was up yet

The chauffeur's compartment in the Phantom VI of 1969. The seat cushion was fixed, for the division was right behind it, built into the backrest. The facia display is similar to that of the latest Silver Shadow, and the chauffeur had his own personal air-conditioning installation.

This is a mid-1970s Phantom VI in a pastel shade and featuring repeater indicators and front-hinged rear doors. In general, the style has not changed for many years.

again, to a total of £12,844; the car established a new record as the first Rolls-Royce to have a basic price in excess of £10,000 (actually it was £10,050). By this time, too, the V8 engine had been given the latest cylinder heads, with the high-mounted sparking plug position, as used on all Silver Shadows, but no difference in performance or power output was ever claimed.

For the first year of Phantom VI production, the cars were given chassis numbers in the same sequence as those being used for Silver Shadows, but from the spring of 1969 the car was allocated a block of its own, though still using the 'standard' PRH . . . prefix. Sales of this car gently declined — only about 50 were delivered in the first year, and by the mid-1970s this figure had dropped further to about 20 cars a year. There has been no resurgence since then, and in the early 1980s it was usual for less than 10 Phantom VIs to be delivered each year from the coachbuilding works in North-West London. The car's prestige, however, is such that Rolls-Royce have kept it in what has virtually become hand-built production, where the economic sourcing of major components like chassis-frames and axle casings must be a nightmare.

From spring 1968 to the beginning of 1978, just 311 $6\frac{1}{4}$-litre Phantom VIs were produced, and in all that time the only major body change was to rehang the rear doors so that they hinged at the front, from the B/C post. Obviously, this was for good safety

reasons, and it was introduced from PRH 4701 in spring 1972. Of those 311 cars, I have been able to identify just five landaulettes.

In the spring of 1978, the Phantom VI's chassis and running gear was thoroughly updated, though the stately body style was left alone. Starting with H.M. The Queen's new car (see below) and in a new chassis sequence PGH . . ., the chassis received the $6\frac{3}{4}$-litre engine which had been a feature of the Silver Shadow since 1970, and the GM400 three-speed, torque converter, automatic transmission, which had been standard on all Silver Shadow derivatives since 1968 (a decade earlier!). At the same time, the venerable transmission-driven mechanical brake servo system was abandoned, the latest Phantom VIs inheriting the high-pressure dual hydraulic circuitry of the Silver Shadow, but still keeping the drum brakes of the original cars. Yet more facia changes kept the cars abreast of the latest Silver Shadows, and the cars were even heavier than before — at least 6,045lb, even before any optional extras were specified.

Small-scale production of the $6\frac{3}{4}$-litre/three-speed cars has been in progress ever since 1978, and I would estimate that less than 50 examples (only two of them landaulettes) had been delivered by mid-1984. No collector, I am sure, will have the opportunity of buying one for some time yet, as their owners seem to keep them for many years. The supply, after all, may

This was the original Phantom V landaulette, constructed by H.J. Mulliner, Park Ward in 1962 for delivery to H.M. The Queen Mother, in which the top folded down from a junction at the top rear of the doors.

When the top was erected there was a very small letter-box-sized rear-view window in the top, and the usual limousine lines were restored almost to normal.

well be running out one day soon! It is significant that *Glass's Guide* (the 'Bible' of the motor trader) makes no mention at all of the Phantom V or Phantom VI, which is just as well, for prices when new were very high, and when secondhand (and well cared-for) are still rather prohibitive.

However, it is worth noting that the new-car price had only risen to £16,058 in late 1973, five years after the Phantom VI had been put on sale, but that by 1976 the car was being built to

Superficially, this 1965 state landaulette from H.J. Mulliner, Park Ward looked like the original 1962 design except for the much larger rear window.

However, in this case the top folded down all the way from the back of the *front* doors, which exposed much more of the rear compartment to the fresh air. The rear quarter-windows on this design were much smaller than on the earlier landaulette.

H.M. The Queen took delivery of two special Park Ward limousine Phantom Vs in 1960 and 1961 — 'Canberra I' and 'Canberra II', in which the roof line, the screen and the window glass, were raised by 5 inches.

special order, and prices were 'on application' . . .

The 'Royal' Phantom Vs and the 'Jubilee' Phantom VI

After H.M. Queen Elizabeth II came to the throne in 1952, she eventually added a second Phantom IV (with straight-eight B80 engine) to that which she had acquired in 1950, but then 'made do' without another new machine until 1960, when the first of three very special Park Ward (later H.J. Mulliner, Park Ward) limousines were delivered. This car, carrying chassis number 5AS33, became known as 'Canberra II', but illogically enough a second car (5AT34) delivered in 1961 was given the name of 'Canberra I'.

Mechanically, the two new Royal Rolls-Royces were standard, which is to say that they had the $6\frac{1}{4}$-litre V8 engine allied to the four-speed Hydramatic transmission, and below the waistline, too, they had standard Park Ward limousine coachwork. What made them truly special, however, was that the roof line was

raised by 5 inches throughout its length. The windscreen, and all the side glass panels, were clearly much deeper to suit.

The rear section of the roof itself — back, top and curved quarters — was panelled in one large transparent Perspex moulding. The remainder of the roof over the rear compartment was in glass, with separate rounded edges above the rear doors in Perspex. All this was to make the occupants more visible on ceremonial occasions, but when privacy was required a steel sliding panel (which stowed in the forward roof panel over the chauffeur) could be moved back, and there were small separate hand-fitted panels over the forward Perspex panels. The large rear Perspex moulding could be obscured by a specially fitted 'dome', a two-part aluminium section, which merged with the rest of the roof lines; this could be fitted up in less than a minute, and it was indicative of Park Ward's attention to detail that there was a $\frac{3}{8}$in gap between Perspex and dome to allow the Perspex to dry out if wet. The rear window in the dome was very small, no

The 'Canberra' Phantom Vs featured Perspex domes over the rear seat, Perspex side panels above the doors and a glass panel in the centre of the roof. All could be covered up to ensure privacy.

The Perspex rear dome of the Phantom V and VI 'Canberras' could be covered by this two-piece light-alloy cover, with a very small rear-view window in the back panel; this cover could be stowed in the boot compartment.

In 1978, the SMM&T, on behalf of the British motor industry, gave this high-roof Phantom VI to H.M. The Queen as a present on the occasion of her Silver Jubilee.

The rear-seat compartment of H.M. The Queen's high-roofed Phantom VI 'Canberra', showing the light-alloy cover in place over the Perspex dome.

more than letter-box size.

Naturally, there were electrically operated windows and division glass (controls being in the central armrest in the rear), separate front and rear radios and full air conditioning. When normally laden, the Canberras were no less than 6ft 1in high, and the extra roof height allowed H.M. The Queen and Prince Philip to enter and alight without having to bend too much.

The two original Canberras have remained in the Royal Mews ever since, and it is highly unlikely that they will ever be sold.

Well in advance of the Queen's Silver Jubliee celebrations, in 1977, the Society of Motor Manufacturers and Traders commissioned a further Phantom (this time a Phantom VI) as a gift on behalf of the British motor industry. However, not even Rolls-Royce Motors are immune from industrial problems and strikes, and the third car was not actually delivered until March 1978. Part of the delay, in fact, was due to the incorporation of all the mechanical improvements later to be made to the most recent series of Phantom VIs — which included the $6\frac{3}{4}$-litre engine, the three-speed GM400 transmission and the high-pressure brake hydraulics.

The latest car used the same high-roof body structure (which has never been made available to *any* other Phantom V or VI customer), this time allied to the four-headlamp nose, and the front-hinged rear passenger doors. Naturally, like the other Royal cars, 'Canberra III' was not registered, and among its unique equipment were special rear compartment fittings, including an extra-wide armrest to accommodate a cassette recorder/player, pushbutton radio and air-conditioning controls. In place of the normal cocktail cabinet, behind the division, was extra cassette stowage and an Asprey clock.

Not only was this car as bulky as the other two Canberras, but it was very much heavier than normal. When revealing the 1978 car to the media, Rolls-Royce quoted an unladen weight of 6,790lb/3,080kg; with a quoted maximum payload of 1,300lb, this meant that under certain conditions it could weigh as much as 8,000lb/3,628kg — still on the standard-section 8.90-15in cross-ply tyres.

This latest car, like others in the Royal Household, not only leads an active and demanding life in the UK, but is often taken overseas for use on state visits, and for that purpose there were special bumper fittings which allowed the blades to be removed quickly and the car's overall length to be reduced by 9 inches for easier stowage in the garage of the Royal Yacht *Britannia*. It is such attention to detail which has always made Rolls-Royce so famous.

This one really does look like Lady Penelope's Rolls-Royce from the TV *Thunderbirds* puppet series! Actually it was a Phantom VI chassis, bodied with convertible coachwork by Frua, and shown at Frankfurt in 1973. The radiator shell, I am sure, is standard Rolls-Royce, while the headlamps come from the Fiat 130 Coupe of the period! Presumably it was bought by a Zurich Gnome?

CHAPTER 5

Bentley R-Type Continental

In the Cricklewood tradition?

The story of the concept, development and production career of the Bentley Continental is now so well-known that I am sure there will be no startling revelations in this and the next chapter. However, I ought to emphasize, as so many other writers have before me, that these cars were not only successful image-builders for Rolls-Royce and Bentley, but were great cars in their own right, and they had a style and a character all of their own. In its first few years, at least, the Bentley Continental was a very important car in the scheme of things at Crewe.

The first Continental could not have been produced at a better time, for at this stage in the life of the 'standard-steel' saloons, the Bentley marque was in urgent need of a marketing boost. The Mk VI saloons, worthy as they were, did not have the same sort of standing as the 'Silent Sports Cars' of the 1930s, and they were obviously not as specialized, nor as exciting, as the massive 'W.O.' Bentleys built at Cricklewood between 1919 and 1931.

Although the first Continental was sold in the summer of 1952, and the decision to build a series on the basis of the Mk VI/R-Type chassis had been taken in 1950, the roots of the development story go back many years earlier than that.

There had never been a 'W.O.' Bentley with the 'Continental' tag in the 1920s and 1930s, for that title had first been given to an exclusive series of rakish-bodied Rolls-Royce 40/50hp Phantom II models in the early 1930s. Later in that decade, the Rolls-Royce development team, led by W.A. Robotham and including Ivan Evernden, became involved in two fast and (for their day) aerodynamically-efficient prototypes — one a factory-inspired four-door saloon on the basis of the Mk V chassis, called 'Corniche', the other a privately-commissioned two-door four-seater with a French Paulin-designed body, now nicknamed 'Embiricos' after the rich Greek who commissioned it on a normal $4\frac{1}{4}$-litre chassis. The 'Corniche' did not survive the war, whereas the 'Embiricos' is in use to this day. Both cars, in the fullness of time, were developed to be more suitable for really fast motoring, and both, to some extent, influenced what was to follow.

Having got the Mark VI Bentley and the Rolls-Royce Silver Dawn well and truly into series production, the design team at Crewe turned their attention to a new project, intended to satisfy the demand for a really fast touring car. For obvious marketing reasons, this would carry a Bentley radiator and badge, and to achieve the speeds envisaged, it would need more power and lower aerodynamic drag. The chassis, except for minor details, would be that of the $4\frac{1}{2}$-litre R-Type Bentley, due to go into production during 1952.

The kernel of the design was a new body style, lower, sleeker and more compact than the four-door 'standard-steel' saloon shape. Although it would eventually be built by the H.J. Mulliner coachbuilding company, the style was originally the work of John Blatchley and Ivan Evernden, at Crewe. They produced quarter-scale models of a two-door, four-seater style, had it tested in the company's wind-tunnel at Hucknall, and found that with a suitably increased power output, a top speed of up to 120mph ought to be possible.

The style, of course, is very well-known, and the pictures reproduced here emphasize the advances made over the standard car. Nevertheless, it is worth noting that a standard style of Bentley radiator grille was retained, although its overall

This Paulin-bodied Bentley, built for one of the Greek Embiricos family in 1938, with much work carried out by Ivan Evernden at Derby, was the spiritual ancestor of the 1952 R-Type Continental.

From this angle, the similarity between the 1938 Paulin-bodied Bentley and the R-Type Continental which was to follow it 14 years later is particularly pronounced. The car was registered in France.

Two years before they were asked to build the production series of R-Type Continentals, H.J. Mulliner had produced this special coupe style for the standard Mk VI chassis, which reveals a slight resemblance.

height was reduced by $1\frac{1}{2}$ inches. Even if the shaping of the flanks and the tail had not been as advanced as it was, this would still have been the smoothest shape to come from Crewe so far, yet there was still seating for four full-sized adults, who had very adequate legroom and headroom. Ivan Evernden, in later life, admitted that for aerodynamic reasons a more sloping nose ('like that of the Volkswagen and of the Citroen' — which means Beetle and DS19, respectively) and the addition of rear wing fins would have made a good shape even better, but there were obvious styling reasons why this would not have been acceptable.

The diligent work which went into the shaping of the car is nevertheless qualified by Evernden, thus: 'Much more could have been done than was done, at the expense of still greater sacrifices, but the purpose of the exercise was to reduce the aero drag of an orthodox car and not to make a space capsule for an astronaut.'

The projected frontal area of the new car, which was originally dubbed 'Corniche II', was 22.1sq ft. The aesthetic appeal of the car speaks for itself, but it is of interest to compare certain key dimensions with those of the R-Type Bentley with which it was a true contemporary:

	R-Type Continental	R-Type saloon
Overall length	17ft 2.5in	16ft 7.5in
Overall width	5ft 11.5in	5ft 9in
Overall height	5ft 3in	5ft 4.5in
Unladen weight	3,700lb	4,060lb
Approx. nett power output	153bhp	140bhp

The very first car, registered OLG 490, and ever afterwards given the nickname 'Olga', had a roof line an inch higher than

The memorable lines of the Bentley R-Type Continental of 1952-55, with coachwork by H.J. Mulliner of Chiswick.

the series-production cars, and was fitted with a divided windscreen, whereas all subsequent cars had a one-piece curved screen. That car, incidentally, originally carried an experimental chassis number, but was given BC26A during 1954, which it still holds.

The suggestion from Evernden to Rolls-Royce management, that 'Corniche II' should be built was made in writing in January 1951, 'Olga' was completed in August 1951, and the car was revealed to the world at the end of February 1952. The first production-car rolling chassis had already been delivered to H.J. Mulliner by this time, and the first delivery, to H. Sentet, in France, was made in June 1952. H.J. Mulliner, though an independent concern at this time, was a logical choice of coachbuilder for these cars, principally because they had developed a very efficient 'lightweight' construction method for limited runs, and because they had already produced a very smart lightweight fastback style on the Mk VI chassis, with some

of the flavour of the Continental about it. The only important change, made in 1951, was that the project title of 'Corniche II' was dropped, and the name 'Continental' took its place. Thus was another distinction between the Bentley and Rolls-Royce marques blurred. The 'Corniche' name would be held in reserve until 1971, when it was applied to the Silver Shadow-based models (coupe *and* convertible, Bentley *and* Rolls-Royce) which H.J. Mulliner were then developing.

After noting that the so-called R-Type Continental went into production in February 1952, four months before the definitive R-Type saloons were built (life is never simple for a historian, even where such a meticulously documented company is concerned!), I can say that few changes were made to the rolling chassis to suit it to this more aerodynamic body style, except that the 4,566cc engines were more powerful, and the overall gearing was considerably higher, together with the use of a much more efficient exhaust system, said to absorb 25bhp less than

OLG 490 — naturally nicknamed 'Olga' — was the prototype R-Type Continental, originally coded 'Corniche II' at the Rolls-Royce factory.

In spite of the sloping lines of the R-Type Continental fastback, there was enough space in the back seats for two adult passengers. Note the front bucket seats.

A 'different' picture, at least, of the R-Type Continental, taken from low down. The number-plate has been blanked out on this print, but the car was almost certainly OLG 490.

standard! (Such sacrifices had to be made on the 'Best Car in the World' to provide ultimate refinement . . .)

Apart from a raised compression ratio of 7.27:1 (which varied slightly during the next two years on different series of engines), the twin-SU-equipped engines were much as before, and the synchromesh transmission was exactly the same, including the familiar right-hand gear-change, with the gear lever tucked down close to the driver's door. The final-drive ratio, however, was much higher at 3.077:1 (that of the saloon was 3.727:1), and there were specially developed 6.50-16in high-speed tyres.

The first few cars, even though exported to the USA and France, had right-hand drive. However, when the time came to start building left-hand-drive Continentals, there was no possibility of providing a left-hand gear-change (this was never developed for the saloons, either). Accordingly, Continental buyers were given the choice of a steering-column gear-change (as in the Rolls-Royce Silver Dawn and left-hand-drive Bentley saloons of the period), or the further option of a central floor change. Five right-hand-drive cars were also equipped with the central change from new.

Although only 208 R-Type Continentals were built in three years — which averages about 70 cars a year, or six cars a month — sales would undoubtedly have been higher if H.J. Mulliner could have produced more bodies. The fact was that this concern had the lion's share of the production chassis, building 193 of the cars. Four other coachbuilders (Park Ward — six, Franay of France — five, Graber — three, and Farina — one) made up the balance. The classic H.J. Mulliner style, therefore, is the shape remembered by nearly all R-Type Continental lovers, and its attraction is mostly due to peerless proportions and delicate detail, rather than decoration. Indeed, there is almost no decoration to be considered, for the overall bulk of the car tells its own story; only the delicate little crease sweeping across the front wings and fading out on the doors could be accused of being a 'styling line'.

As with many other special bodies built for use on these chassis, construction at the Chiswick works started on the basis of a standard floorpan, but every other metal panel was in light alloy, and at first a great deal of attention went into the making of light seats, door hardware and other fittings. Nowhere in the

According to Rolls-Royce records, no R-Type Continental was ever originally bodied by Abbott of Farnham — yet this car is said to have an Abbott bodyshell from 1952-53. Any offers?

shell, except on the facia panel, was any wood used. The facia, of course, was completely different in layout from the Mk VI saloon, though the same instruments found themselves in revised locations. Because this was potentially such a high-performance car, there was a rev-counter to match the speedometer, both of these large-diameter dials finding themselves behind the steering wheel, in line with the driver's eyes. Considering the shape of the bodyshell and the graceful sweep of the roof down to a long tail, rear-seat accommodation was remarkably generous, and the boot itself was almost as spacious as that of the saloon.

Almost as soon as the R-Type Continental was put on the market, customer demands began to erode its specification. Conceived originally as a lightweight car (the bodyshells weighed only about 730lb at first), it gradually put on weight over the years — items like heavier seats, more and plusher fittings being the principal culprits in the process. By 1955, some

bodies weighed as much as 1,050lb, and total weight could approach 4,000lb.

Production got under way slowly, and only nine production cars were delivered before the R-Type saloon was put on show at Earls Court in October 1952. By this time, *The Autocar* had tested 'Olga', confirming Rolls-Royce's claims for the car with a top speed of 115.4mph, 0-60mph acceleration in 13.5 seconds and 0-100mph in 36.0 seconds. The testers also achieved 19.4mpg over a long and vigorous test during August 1952. Not for nothing did they sum up the car: 'This Bentley is a modern magic carpet which annihilates great distances and delivers the occupants well-nigh as fresh as when they started. It is a car Britain may well be proud of, and it is sure to add new lustre to the name it bears.' If, I ought to add, one could afford the price, for the R-Type Continental's total UK price at this time was £7,608, which compared with a mere £4,824 asked for the standard R-Type saloon. That difference of £2,784 would buy

SMA 410 denotes an R-Type Continental originally registered in Cheshire in 1954. It was, in fact, the company demonstrator for a time, with the standard H.J. Mulliner body style.

Some R-Type Continentals had rear wheel spats, some not. The car looked good in either condition.

several other mundane cars at that time, so no wonder demand was strictly limited!

The performance of the R-Type Continental, 'magic carpet' or not, needs to be put into perspective today, where its performance and cross-country abilities would be absolutely annihilated by cars like the Ford Escort XR3i or the VW Golf GTi, to name just two contemporary examples. Yes, I know . . . the R-Type Continental offered a completely unique type of motoring, and it was a very fast car of its day. But don't go out

and buy one today and expect to keep up with the thrusters in their mass-produced 2-litre saloons and hatchbacks! Automatic transmission was introduced for the saloon cars from the autumn of 1952, but was not made available in the R-Type Continentals for some time after that, probably because it was thought that the customers would not want it. The first four automatic-transmission cars, mated to the existing 4,566cc engines, were not delivered until April 1954, and in fact there were only six such combinations in all.

Even before the R-Type Continental had been put on the market, Rolls-Royce had started testing the final stretch of the B60 engine, in which the cylinder bore had been enlarged to 95.25mm/3.75in and the swept volume had become 4,887cc, but the cylinder head, porting and valve sizes were unchanged. This, however, was only an interim development, for with the new Silver Cloud/S-Series in mind, the company also proposed to develop an entirely new cylinder head casting, with individual inlet ports.

However, to counteract the inexorable increase in vehicle weights found as R-Type Continental production evolved, it was decided to put the 'interim' 4,887cc engine into these cars, even though it was never made available in the ordinary Rolls-Royce or Bentley saloons. The chassis number noters will want to know that it was fitted to a total of 82 cars, from May 1954 (in the 'D' and 'E' series) and I think it is significant that of these, no fewer than 36 also had automatic transmission. Peak power, as usual, was not stated, but we might estimate 165bhp, at best.

Even though the Continental was expensive and exclusive (and was always meant to be so), its popularity increased as its

Nose detail of the R-Type Continental, complete with lowered radiator shell and extra driving lamps for use in fog.

The rear style of the H.J. Mulliner-bodied R-Type Continental featured a long, smooth sweep over the rear window to the rear bumper. The notched line under the wheel spats of this particular car is an individual touch.

virtues became known. Production was building up all the time, and it is interesting to see that 51 cars, or almost a quarter of total R-Type Continental sales, were delivered from January to May 1955, just as the car was about to be replaced. That momentum would be carried forward, with interest, to the S-Series cars which followed.

Before the end, too, Rolls-Royce made one major policy change, concerning the supply of bodies for Continental chassis. At first the 'standard' H.J. Mulliner shell was used on every car, and it was not until the spring of 1954 that this monopoly was broken. R-Type Continentals were then bodied by Franay (in France), Graber (in Switzerland) and Farina (Italy), but these were really only sideshows; the real significance was the arrival of Park Ward on the scene.

At first, Rolls-Royce had kept their Park Ward subsidiary well away from the R-Type Continental project, but with the S-Series cars due in 1955 they changed their strategy. More Continental sales were planned for this car, and because the limit would always be defined by the number of bodies which could be made, it was decided to duplicate the sources. Henceforward, therefore, both Mulliner and Park Ward would build special coachbuilt shells for this chassis.

In 1954 and 1955, Park Ward built just six cars (four drophead coupes and two saloons). The style and the structure of these cars, however, was exactly the same as would be offered on the S-Series chassis to follow. Below the waistline and behind the windscreen, of course, the drophead and saloon shells were essentially identical.

Compared with the H.J. Mulliner style, the Park Ward design was rather more squared-up, rather more formal, and slightly less 'sporting'. There was no H.J. Mulliner drophead derivative,

in any case. One feature of the Park Ward style was the vestigial fins at the rear of each rear wing, and two-tone paintwork was also offered.

The Park Ward saloon bodyshell, if anything, was slightly lighter than that of the H.J. Mulliner, and the drophead coupe derivative was 50 to 80lb lighter than that, for Park Ward had been pioneers of all-metal construction way back in the mid-1930s, and knew all about weight-saving. The real miracle, however, was that this same basic bodyshell was also used on the S-Series chassis which followed, even though it had a 3-inch longer wheelbase and 2-inch wider wheel tracks! Only a close inspection shows where changes to the style and the structure had to be made, the shape of the rear wheelarches and rear wing profile giving one clue.

On the R-Type Continental chassis, however, five of the six Park Ward cars built had the 4,887cc engine, three of them with automatic transmission, and no less than four of these cars were originally built for display at motor shows in the autumn of 1954. We might assume, I feel, that all the R-Type Park Ward shells count as 'pre-production', really a try-out for the S-Series cars which were to follow.

I am indebted to Stanley Sedgwick's booklet, produced by the Bentley Drivers Club in 1978, for much of the information in this chapter, especially for the encouraging news that nearly 170 of the 208 cars built are still known to exist (including five of the Park Ward-bodied cars). There is no doubt that of all the splendid cars reviewed in this volume, the R-Type Continental is the one which has built up an exceptional reputation and mystique. Even so, the S-Series Continental which followed outsold it and outlasted it, even though it was by no means as special. The story of these cars follows in the next chapter.

CHAPTER 6

Bentley S-Type Continental
Six-cylinder and V8 versions

In the lengthy period covered by this book and its companion volume, the most important of several major changes occurred in the spring of 1955. For Rolls-Royce Ltd, at Crewe, this was the point at which the nine-year career of the Mk VI/R-Type/Silver Dawn models came to an end, and at which the new Silver Clouds and S-Series models were ushered into the limelight. Although we did not know it at the time, these cars would hold the stage for more than 10 years, after which the first-ever monocoque Rolls-Royce would be put on sale.

In 1955, therefore, there was change in all directions — technically, in marketing and in manufacturing terms. Naturally, when the 'standard-steel' saloon line changed over, Bentley Continental build smoothly followed suit. The last R-Type Continental rolling chassis left Crewe on February 18, 1955 (and was bodied at H.J. Mulliner by the end of April), while the first S1 Continental chassis followed it on March 29.

However, there was a considerable delay before the existence of an S-Type Continental was confirmed, not only to allow the last of the now-obsolete R-Type Continentals to be delivered, but because H.J. Mulliner needed some time to prepare for a new body style. Park Ward, as I have pointed out in the last chapter, had already tried out their new shell on a few R-Type chassis, but there had been no change from H.J. Mulliner since 1952. The S-Type Continental, in the event, was officially launched in September 1955, with the first deliveries following a few days later.

As I have already described the new S-Series chassis design in some detail in the companion volume, at this point I need only state the differences provided for the new Continental derivatives. The new frame, of course, had box-section main members and a massive cruciform section in the centre, semi-trailing independent front suspension, and 'Z-bar' location of the rear axle, allied to a 10ft 3in wheelbase and a 5ft 0in rear track, respectively 3 inches and 2 inches larger than on the obsolete chassis. The RR/GM four-speed automatic transmission had been standardized on all cars (though a manual option would remain on S-Type Continentals for the first year or so), and the familiar type of hydro-mechanical braking system, with transmission-driven mechanical servo, also remained in evidence.

More important than the bald statement of facts and figures was the improved packaging — lengthwise at least — of the new design, where the radiator had been moved forward, and the engine and transmission with it, the result being more space from toeboard under the facia to the rear axle. Overall, therefore, the new S-Type Continentals could be more spacious without being much longer, although inevitably they would be heavier than before. Compared with the 3,700lb of an early R-Type Continental, the weight of an early S1 Continental would be 4,250lb, and even this would creep up a little over the years; by 1960, a four-door James Young shell, as tested by *The Autocar*, would weigh no less than 4,460lb at the kerbside. It was no wonder that the S-Type Continentals were never quicker than the original lightweight R-Types had been, or that the R-Types have always been preferred by true high-performance enthusiasts.

At a time when the new 'standard-steel' saloons had 4,887cc and new cylinder heads, but a 6.6:1 compression ratio, the S1

H.J. Mulliner's S-Type Continental, introduced in the autumn of 1955, was very similar indeed to the original R-Type and certainly used some common panels. This particular car had the 4.9-litre six-cylinder engine.

The S-Type Continental, like its R-Type counterpart, had a long, wide, but very shallow boot compartment. This was the tail of the H.J. Mulliner-bodied example. Note the tail lamps, which were also used on the Park Ward-bodied Alvis TD21 body.

Continental engine had a 7.25:1 compression ratio. Apart from the short-lived possibility of ordering a car with the old synchromesh transmission, the S1 Continental customer was also provided with smaller-section tyres (7.60 instead of 8.20 section at first), and the very high final-drive ratio of 2.923:1 compared with 3.42:1 for the 'standard-steel' saloon.

When sales officially began in the autumn of 1955, there was a choice of three body styles on the same chassis — the drophead coupe and saloon styles from Park Ward, which had already been seen on the last of the R-Types, along with a new H.J. Mulliner saloon shape, all with two passenger doors and full four-seater accommodation.

The new H.J. Mulliner style was visually very close to that of the classic R-Type (I suspect that quite a few common panels were retained), though the wing lines swept more smoothly through from nose to tail, the crease emphasis now went all the way to the tail, and the radiator shell stood slightly further forward in relation to the front wheels.

The factory, of course, provided the chassis complete with floorpan and scuttle/bulkhead/facia. The facia itself was

The S-Type Continental by H.J. Mulliner has a very fully-equipped instrument panel. The car, like almost all Continentals, had automatic transmission.

The registration number is misleading, for this certainly is not a 1964 S-Type Continental model. The H.J. Mulliner shell is of the original S-Type, and clearly has something in common with the obsolete R-Type.

different from the old R-Type layout and completely different, too, from that of the latest saloons. All the dials were grouped ahead of the driver's eyes, behind the steering wheel, with a rev-counter still much in evidence.

Incidentally, although H.J. Mulliner (with 218 bodies) and Park Ward (185 bodies) took most of the business for S1 Continentals, James Young bodied 20 cars, Hooper six and Graber and Franay one each (though these last, I am sure, were for old time's sake, rather than with any serious intent in mind).

Changes made to the standard chassis were also made to the S1 Continentals at about the same time, which is to say that power-assisted steering started to appear in 1956 (for UK customers this feature was delayed until the autumn of the year), and was standardized in 1958, along with other less obvious improvements. In 1956, too, there was an important improvement to the engine (from chassis BC21BG, the first car so equipped), in which the compression ratio was increased to 8:1, larger (2in choke) SU carburettors and larger inlet valves were specified, and peak power rose to what we now know was 178bhp (nett).

In 1957, too, the company made another marketing concession, and for the first time put a Continental chassis on sale with a four-door saloon body style, by H.J. Mulliner. There was a mealy-mouthed period when we were all supposed to call this derivative a 'Flying Spur' (after the family crest of the Arthur Johnstone clan, Johnstone being H.J.M's Managing Director at the time) and forget all about the Continental chassis underneath, but this was speedily forgotten. Rolls-Royce Ltd, it seems, had been rather stuffy about the use of the 'Continental' title, insisting that it be applied only to two-door cars, with light weight and low wind-resistance, and it took much patient nagging from H.J. Mulliner to allow the 'Flying Spur' and 'Continental' titles to appear in the same brochure, which eventually they did.

The Flying Spur four-door style was largely the result of co-operation between Mulliner's chief stylist, Herbert Nye, and the Blatchley/Evernden project team at Crewe. It retained the lowered Continental radiator shell and some of the front-end panelling of the two-door saloon's shell, but while the side/wing profiles and the tail were superficially like the two-door, the centre section and the roof were rejigged to allow for four passenger doors and a rear quarter-window behind the rear passenger door. Naturally there was a more pronounced notchback effect at the tail, and a generous luggage boot was provided.

Once Rolls-Royce had removed their embargo on the use of four-door saloon shells on the S1 chassis, James Young and Hooper followed suit, and — just to cause confusion — H.J. Mulliner also produced a drophead coupe version of their two-door saloon style, but used a Rolls-Royce radiator and did not offer it on the Continental chassis!

The prices, at this point, were interesting. At the 1957 show,

Despite the 1964 registration number, this car has a pre-1963 single-headlamp type of H.J. Mulliner's S-Type Continental body.

H.J. Mulliner's alternative to the S-Type (S1) Continental coupe was this attractive drophead coupe, which used many of the same panels. There was also a Rolls-Royce-radiatored derivative on the 'standard-steel' chassis.

total UK prices were as follows:

Bentley S1 'standard-steel' saloon	£5,544
Continental 2-dr saloon (H.J. Mulliner)	£7,914
Continental 2-dr saloon (Park Ward)	£7,494
Continental 2-dr drophead (Park Ward)	£7,494
Flying Spur 4-dr saloon (H.J. Mulliner)	£7,994
Flying Spur-type James Young 4-dr	£7,884
Flying Spur-type Hooper 4-dr	£7,966

In the summer of 1959, of course, there was a further upheaval, not only because H.J. Mulliner and Park Ward both changed their styling on the same basic chassis, but because Rolls-Royce finally introduced their light-alloy V8 6,230cc engine to replace the six-cylinder B60-type unit. There were a few final S1 Continentals fitted with the modified H.J. Mulliner two-door saloon bodyshell, which was basically as before, but had a wrap-around rear window and different tail lamps, but this shell was really destined for more general use on the S2.

Chassis improvements for the latest Continental, which became the S2 model, now included the use of the compact, lightweight, 6¼-litre V8, which produced about 200bhp in its original state (although this was never officially confirmed), but there was power-assisted steering as standard equipment, and the boot-mounted refrigeration/air-conditioning system continued to be optional. First seen in 1956, this system was replaced on 'standard-steel' S2s by a new installation with the main bulk of conditioning in the front wing, behind the right-hand wheel; there was no space for the new system in the S2 Continental bodies, so the original was retained.

Also new for the S2 Continentals (and not adopted for the 'standard-steel' saloons) were improved front brakes, which

From 1959, with the arrival of the S2 Continental, complete with 6¼-litre V8 engine, H.J. Mulliner modified the styling of their usual two-door bodyshell to include a wraparound rear window and a notch rather than a fastback. . .

... and from the autumn of 1962 the same shell was upgraded to S3 condition with the help of four headlamps.

effectively had four half-shoes, or more precisely two half-friction shoes per main shoe plate. Drum sizes were unchanged from the S1, but the total lining area had been increased from 240sq in to 300sq in. For the first time, too, on this Girling brake, there was automatic adjustment for lining wear.

To the onlooker, of course, the most obvious changes were to the body styles. The H.J. Mulliner style was that already seen on the last S1s, and to the relief of many there were none of the excesses (notably sharp rear fins and complex extra side-lamp housings atop the front wings) which had been seen on the prototype, the 'Continental Special' shown at the end of 1958. For the S2 shell, too, the radiator grille had been moved 2 inches further forward, and canted slightly forward as well. (H.J. Mulliner were really far too preoccupied with the finalization of the 'beheaded' Silver Cloud/S2 convertible, for introduction at the same 1959 motor shows, to do more than this to a well-liked body style.)

The major new style, however, came from Park Ward, who dropped their graceful shell after five successful years, and introduced a brand new and striking drophead coupe with a new and distinctive 'straight through' wing crown line, which linked discreet headlamp hoods directly to the tail lamp cluster housing. It was the first-ever 'straight through' style to be offered for a car from Crewe, and it was to remain on sale until the early months of 1966. Not only would it be a 'standard' Continental style for more than six years, but it would also turn up, occasionally, with a Rolls-Royce radiator on the conventional Silver Cloud chassis!

To match the new skin lines there was a smart new facia layout, with all instruments mounted in a hooded nacelle ahead of the steering wheel. The windscreen featured considerable wrap-around, the radiator shell was even shorter than before (3 inches lower than the saloon equivalent) and further forward, as in the latest H.J. Mulliner style. The main floorpan, scuttle and some inner panels were in pressed steel, the rest of the shells being fashioned from light alloy, with no wood anywhere except on the facia itself. *The Motor* described this body construction in a short feature at announcement time, pointing out that such bodies were no longer hand-crafted, and that the majority of panels were produced in small batches on a stretcher press, a

A beautifully preserved S2 Continental, complete with wraparound rear window, and Alvis-type rear light cluster (or should I call the Alvis lights 'Bentley type'?). In spite of the swooping roof line there was ample room for four adults.

A direct comparison between two H.J. Mulliner body styles in 1957 — the two-door S-Type Continental and the closely-related four-door Flying Spur saloon which, at first, Rolls-Royce did not want to be called 'Continental'.

The original Flying Spur Bentley, by H.J. Mulliner, had rear quarters like this, allied to sizeable rear quarter-windows . . .

. . . but by the time the S3 Continental was launched, the Flying Spur had been given smaller rear quarter-windows and more sheet metal behind them.

This Park Ward drophead coupe bodyshell was introduced for the last of the R-Type Continentals in 1954, then slightly modified to allow for the longer wheelbase and wider tracks of the S-Type Continental, and was used until autumn 1959. It was a full four-seater, of course, with a 115mph top speed.

technique first pioneered in the aircraft industry, where quantities of panels were similarly low.

On announcement, therefore, there was a factory-approved choice of five different bodyshells for the S2 Continental chassis — the H.J. Mulliner Flying Spur four-door and the revised two-door saloons, the new Park Ward drophead coupe, along with four-door saloon and two-door coupe styles from James Young. Prices varied from £8,246 for the Park Ward offering to £8,714 for the James Young four-door. All but the James Young two-door style appeared in the sales catalogue, and it was interesting to see not only how each type had an easily recognizable look of its own, but how each had something special to offer. From Park Ward it was the convertible roof and the modern styling, from H.J. Mulliner it was the exclusive four-door Flying Spur shape,

and from James Young it was a subtly different and more rounded four-door shape with more glass area.

Nor was there any doubt about the appeal of this range. In four years, a total of 431 S1 Continentals had been sold (110 a year, approximately), whereas in three years there would be 388 S2 Continentals (or about 130 a year); the new styles had something to take pride in, but it was the unseen attraction of the new V8 engine which did most for the image. This, too, in spite of a slight hitch in converting from S1 to S2 production, for the last S1 Continental was delivered to the coachbuilder on April 10, 1959, whereas the first S2 Continental did not leave Crewe until July 24.

It is interesting to note that from this point there was really little difference between the Continental and the 'standard-

Bird's-eye view of the Park Ward S1 Continental drophead coupe with hood erect. The lines look good from every angle.

One of the very rare Graber-bodied S-Type Continentals, seen at the Geneva motor show of 1957. Note the headlamps and the extra driving lamps in the corners of the front wings.

In the autumn of 1959, Park Ward introduced the very first 'straight-through' wing style for Bentley Continentals, which hid the S2 chassis and the V8 engine. In this guise it was only sold as a drophead coupe, which looked as neat as a closed coupe with the padded hood erect.

The passenger compartment of the 'straight-through'-style Park Ward Continental drophead coupe showing off four full-size seats and excellent access to the rear seats through the large doors.

For 1963, all Rolls-Royce and Bentley chassis inherited the S3 specification and four-headlamp noses, so Park Ward (now, properly, H.J. Mulliner, Park Ward) modified their existing style very neatly indeed.

steel' chassis, for the S2 saloon's final-drive gearing had been raised to 3.08:1 (nearly, but not quite, as high as that of the S2 Continental) and the tyres were now virtually the same size; only the unique braking installation, just described, made any real difference. Nonetheless, there was always the distinction of having a fast Bentley with special coachwork — although you could theoretically buy a special style on a 'standard-steel' chassis, there was really no point any more, in fact in three years of S2 production, only 15 'beheaded' H.J. Mulliner conversions were built, and none from other companies.

H.J. Mulliner built 221 of the S2 Continental shells, many of them Flying Spur four-door saloons, while Park Ward built 125 cars (all the smart new drophead coupes) and James Young built 41 cars. The only 'private venture' body came from Hooper, who built a single four-door saloon immediately before they closed their doors at the end of 1959.

Finally, in the autumn of 1962, the S2 gave way to the S3 Continental, falling into line with what was being offered on the standard saloons. The V8 engine's power was increased because it was given a higher, 9:1 compression ratio, with 2in choke SU

In 1963, for the first time, there was a fixed-head coupe derivative of the drophead illustrated on the previous page with a rather angular top.

carburettors (except for certain export markets) and the various bodyshells were given four headlamps, though not always the same lamps as those now standard on the saloons and the Phantom V limousine.

In the meantime, too, Rolls-Royce Ltd, having taken over H.J. Mulliner in the summer of 1959, merged that business with Park Ward in 1961, the result being that the new subsidiary became known as H.J. Mulliner, Park Ward. In the fullness of time the old Chiswick works was closed down, and all body coachbuilding was concentrated in London NW10.

For 1963, in S3 four-headlamp form, the H.J. Mulliner Flying Spur four-door and the alternative two-door saloon continued as before, along with the James Young four-door saloon and the Park Ward two-door drophead coupe (which now had a Rolls-Royce equivalent). In addition, however, Park Ward also offered a two-door saloon, which was effectively a hardtop version of the 'straight through' bodyshell, with a metal roof, a relatively flat rear window, and large quarter-windows alongside the rear seats. The only option to disappear was the James Young two-door offering. For the first time, incidentally, Rolls-Royce had

James Young of Bromley produced this very smart and sleek four-door bodyshell for the S2 Continental chassis which . . .

. . . was carried on for 1963 with the obligatory four-headlamp nose.

The interior of the H.J. Mulliner Flying Spur body, as introduced in 1957, revealing the generous depth of the seat cushions.

achieved uniformity in pricing, for the 1963 Continentals all cost £7,861 — saloon, two-door, or drophead coupe (the S3 saloon cost £5,384 at the time). A Purchase Tax cut in November 1962 had been very useful, for this made the cars significantly cheaper than at the start of S2 Continental production four years earlier!

The S3 Continental, like the standard saloons on which it was based, now settled down into a gentle decline. Between July 1962, when the first S3 chassis was delivered, and November 1965 (three months after S3 saloon deliveries had ended), when the last went off to Mulliner, Park Ward to be bodied, 312 S3 Continentals were built. Of these, Mulliner, Park Ward produced 291, with James Young producing 20 shells and Graber building just a single car. Incidentally, although the graceful, but ageing, H.J. Mulliner two-door saloon was originally listed as an S3 body option, it disappeared from the price lists well before the end of 1962; it seems doubtful that it

was ever built in series in four-headlamp form.

Production of S3 Continentals did not end in the summer of 1965, as originally planned, the final few cars being manufactured at Crewe from August to November 1965 to help tide over the Crewe production lines pending the late build-up of Silver Shadow assembly. The last S3 Continental of all was delivered to the dockside, for shipment to an overseas customer, at the end of January 1966. It was the end of a distinguished 14-year career for a famous model derivative.

The name 'Continental' has now been revived on the latest Bentley coachbuilt model, previously called 'Corniche' as at the time of writing, in 1984. There are those who think it should have been applied to a high-performance alternative to the Pininfarina-styled Rolls-Royce Camargue, and others who think it would have been a better name than 'Mulsanne Turbo'. Perhaps we'd just better wait and see what happens . . .

CHAPTER 7

From Mk VI to Series S3

Special coachwork on 'standard-steel' chassis

I have already related how Rolls-Royce's policy towards bodyshell construction changed between the mid-1930s and the mid-1940s — how the company first came to rely on batch production of similar shells from companies like Park Ward, and how it was decided to put a complete car (bodyshell and all) on to the market after the Second World War.

Top management, however, was not foolish enough to think that this marketing upheaval would be accepted by all their potential customers and dealers. Accordingly, they always made sure that the new production lines at Crewe could either supply complete cars (with Pressed Steel Company bodies), or rolling chassis for despatch to a coachbuilder chosen by the customer. The fact that this was likely to cost a buyer much more, and delay his receipt of the completed vehicle by several months, was no deterrent — the customer was always right, of course!

W.A. Robotham's belief, that the 'standard-steel' bodyshell would eventually be accepted by almost every customer, was proved conclusively in the long run — but it was a very long run! Right through from 1946, when the first coachbuilt Bentley Mk VI was completed, to 1966, when the very last coachbuilt Rolls-Royce Silver Cloud III was delivered, there was always an alternative to the standard style.

Even so, the statistics show without a doubt that demand for individual shells dropped considerably in the first 10 postwar years, and disappeared almost completely before production of the separate-chassis Rolls-Royce and Bentley cars came to an end. The customers, it seemed, soon got out of the old habit of wanting a hand-built bodyshell to complement their hand-made shoes, their Savile Row suits and their specially constructed

guns. One set of figures, for cars carrying the Bentley radiator, proves this most graphically. Between 1946 and 1952, no fewer than 999 Mk VIs were supplied with specialist coachwork (19% of total production), compared with just 145 Sls (4.6%) and just two S3 examples. Even the cachet of the Rolls-Royce radiator did not tip the balance towards special styles, for of the 761 Silver Dawns built between 1949 and 1955, there were only 66 cars with special body styles.

One reason, of course, was that social standards were changing all the time, another was that the cost of employing skilled craftsmen had shot up since the war, and a third, following on from these, was that fewer and fewer major coachbuilders were still in operation.

It is interesting to compare the coachbuilders' roll-call in the mid-1930s, when sales of Rolls-Royce and Bentley chassis from Derby were at their height, and the situation in the mid-1950s, when the number of coachbuilt body styles had almost entirely disappeared. In 1935, Arnold, Barker, Cockshoot, Freestone & Webb, Hooper, Mann Egerton, Arthur Mulliner, H.J. Mulliner, Gurney Nutting, Park Ward, Rippon, Thrupp & Maberly, Vanden Plas, Windovers and James Young all had special styles to show at the Olympia Motor Show. In 1955, however, the situation was very different, with only Freestone & Webb, H.J. Mulliner, Hooper, Park Ward, Harold Radford and James Young in evidence. Five years later, Freestone & Webb had closed down — as had Hooper — H.J. Mulliner had been taken over by Rolls-Royce for amalgamation with Park Ward, while Harold Radford had virtually abandoned Rolls-Royce/Bentley work altogether.

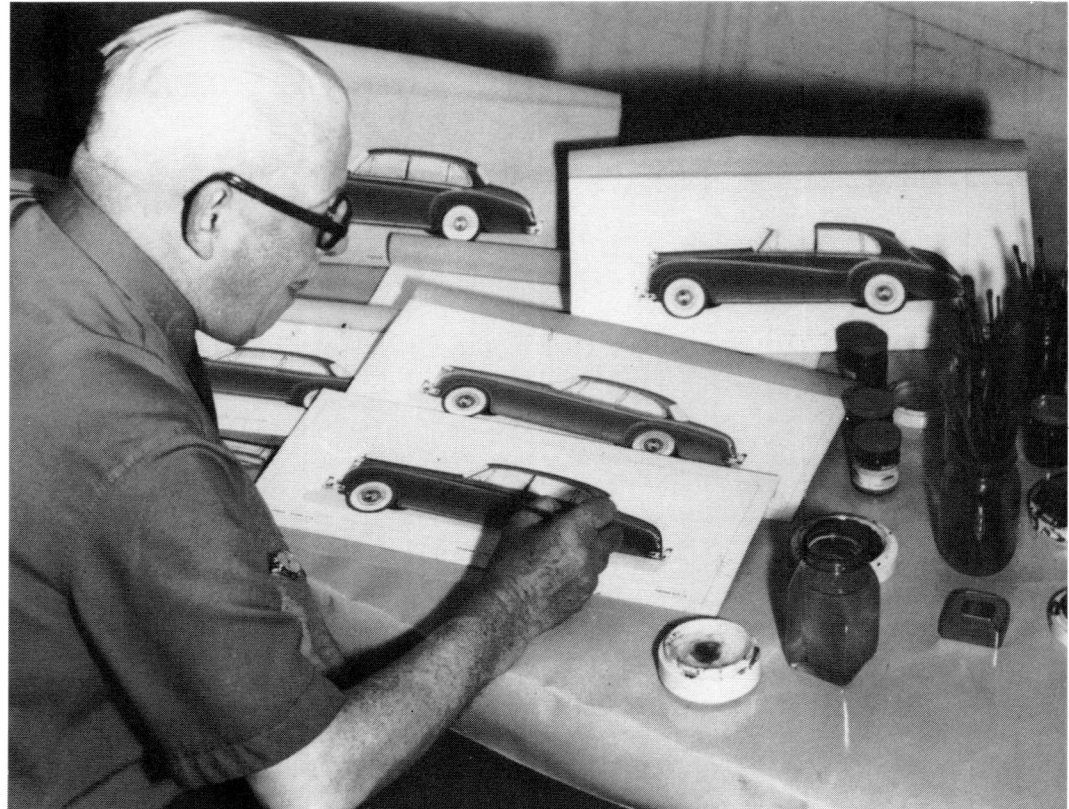

In the halcyon days of coachbuilding, a specialist would prepare several colour renderings for submission to his client, who would then choose the bodyshell for his particular car. This shot was taken at James Young in the early 1960s.

In the immediate postwar years, however, specialist coachwork on the standard Mk VI chassis was very popular, not only because there was a vast pent-up demand for new cars after six years of war, but because Rolls-Royce could produce more rolling chassis than complete cars. Rationing applied to steel sheet, rather than to castings and forgings, so the company could only build so many complete cars, many of which had to be exported to ensure future supplies. It followed that much of the metal going into the postwar breed of coachbuilt Bentley was light alloy.

It was a measure of surviving tradition that, when the Mk VI Bentley was revealed in May 1946, the motoring press carried display advertisements from Hooper, Park Ward and Vanden Plas showing sketches of new styles, while retailers like Jack Barclay, Car Mart and University Motors all majored on the idea of a Bentley with special coachwork.

Because there was a short delay in building up body supplies from Pressed Steel (and ensuring that they were of appropriate quality), the company managed to supply rolling chassis to coachbuilders well before the first 'standard-steel' cars were delivered. The first actually left Crewe in February 1946, three months before the existence of the new model was confirmed,

Before Harold Radford turned to building high-quality conversions of standard bodies, he produced special coachwork like this estate car on the Mk VI Bentley chassis.

In 1951, Harold Radford produced one of his first Bentley Countryman conversions. The rear-quarter treatment, perhaps, is a little clumsy.

Two views of the Rolls-Royce Silver Dawn, as converted to hatchback/estate car status by the Harold Radford combine. This particular car was built in 1954.

In 1948, Farina produced this two-door Continental coupe on the basis of the Mk VI Bentley . . .

. . . whereas in 1949, the same coach-builder showed this more conventional four-seater drophead coupe on the same chassis.

Ghia, still an independent concern in those days, produced this very impressive four-door saloon on the Rolls-Royce Silver Dawn chassis in 1952.

and home market deliveries of both types began at the same time, in September 1946. The first coachbuilt Mk VI to be exported to the USA — a James Young saloon — went to the shipper at the end of February 1947.

After the initial burst, however, the proportion of specially-clad Mk VIs began to decline. This, in some ways, was helped along by the difficulty some stylists had in blending modern trends in shapes with the traditional needs of their wealthy (and often quite old-fashioned) clientele. It did not help them that Rolls-Royce would normally only supply a rolling chassis on the understanding that the standard radiator shell, scuttle/bulkhead and wheel trims would be retained.

At the first postwar Earls Court Motor Show, for instance, Gurney Nutting showed a striking sedanca-coupe, with real exposed hood-folding irons, which looked dignified without looking odd, while James Young, of all people, showed a two-door 'saloon-coupe' with plain full-width panelling, which looked somewhat like a stretched Standard Vanguard, or a smoothed-out Plymouth. It was not a success. The Hooper sports saloon (for £5,967) was much more successful, though it looked remarkably similar to the 'standard-steel' saloon, no doubt because *that* car had been inspired by late-1930s Hooper razor-

This lightweight four-door saloon body style by H.J. Mulliner, seen at several motor shows in the early 1950s, was said to be the principal inspiration behind the shaping of the Rolls-Royce Silver Cloud which followed. One can easily see why.

At the first postwar British Motor Show — at Earls Court in 1948 — and shortly before they went out of business, Gurney Nutting showed this unique type of two-door sedanca de ville shell on the Mk VI chassis . . .

. . . the alternative being to have the same car without opera windows, but with false hood irons.

In some ways, E.D. Abbott was an underestimated coachbuilder, as this 1952 R-Type Bentley creation confirms.

edge styles!

Two or three years later, the styling trends had settled down, and coachbuilt Mk VIs, R-Types and Silver Dawns had begun to look dignified and serene, often only slightly smaller than the Silver Wraiths, which all had special coachwork. Park Ward's all-metal construction was being copied (as closely as patents would allow) by companies like H.J. Mulliner, and it was a 'lightweight' Mulliner four-door sports saloon, seen over a period of years, which quite clearly influenced the styling of the Silver Cloud, which was to be revealed a few years hence.

Specially-clothed versions of the 'standard-steel' cars tended to be much more expensive than the ordinary versions, because of the hundreds of hours craftsmen needed to erect the shells, and because of the time the bodyshell spent inhabiting expensive floor space. Purely as an example, I quote prices from the autumn of 1953, by which time the Rolls-Royce Silver Dawn had been released for home-market sale alongside the equivalent

Bentley, the R-Type. These were as follows:

Bentley R-Type standard saloon	£4,393
— with Mulliner 4-dr saloon body	£5,937
— with Park Ward 2-dr dhc body	£6,064
— with James Young 4-dr saloon body	£6,284
Rolls-Royce Silver Dawn standard saloon	£4,605
— with Park Ward 2-dr dhc body	£6,277

I need hardly add that the same Park Ward shell, for instance, was used with the choice of Bentley or Rolls-Royce radiator, but with exactly the same fittings and embellishments in each case; the price mark-up compared with the standard saloon car was the same for both types.

Most of the coachbuilders liked to indulge themselves with the production of entirely special shells, but Messrs Harold Radford (Coachbuilders) Ltd, of London NW10 (amazing, wasn't it, how many companies clustered in that far-from-patrician corner of

How many graceful Hooper cars had that company's unmistakable rear-quarter treatment in the ate 1940s and early 1950s? This model was on the basis of a Bentley Mk VI chassis.

See caption on next page.

Three variations on a theme by Freestone & Webb, all on the Mk VI or R-Type chassis. The 1951 example on the previous page had two-tone treatment allied to pronounced rear wheelarches, the 1952 example above showed a longer tail and a complete lack of wheelarch bulges, and by 1954 that same bodyshell had been given much larger rear quarter-windows (below).

H.J. Mulliner tried this 'straight-through' wing line on a Bentley Mk VI chassis in 1948, but it was not a success.

Headlamps recessed into the front wings were an uncharacteristic feature for a Bentley from the early-postwar period. This drophead coupe was photographed at Duxford in 1984.

James Young's special-bodied Mk VI Bentley of 1951, with lines typical of other cars being made at Bromley at the time.

London?) specialized in their Countryman conversions, where the lines of the 'standard-steel' saloon were retained, but modifications might include the construction of a hatchback conversion (or perhaps I should say 'shooting brake' conversion), rear seats could be made to fold, and all manner of useful country-sport equipment (fishing rods, guns, shooting sticks, golfing umbrellas) were fitted into special compartments.

Following the launch of the Silver Cloud and the Bentley S-Series in 1955, the number of coachbuilt alternatives on the basis of the standard chassis decreased yet again. The trend, in any case, had accelerated after the Bentley R-Type Continental was launched in 1952 and, once the S-Type Continental appeared in the autumn of 1955, nearly all the special construction was concentrated on that chassis type. In 10 years from 1955 to 1965, there were 1,131 S-Type Continentals and just 162 specially-clothed standard chassis.

By the end of the 1950s, in any case, Freestone & Webb and Hooper had both pulled out of the coachbuilding business, while Park Ward had also abandoned work on the standard chassis. Park Ward, having started building for the Bentley Continental in 1954, for the long-wheelbase Silver Cloud limousine in 1957 and for the Alvis contract in 1958, were far too busy to do anything else, which left only H.J. Mulliner and James Young to deal with this limited business.

H.J. Mulliner first produced a handsome four-door saloon in its well-known 'lightweight' construction, complete with alloy structure under the sleek skin, which had similar lines to the Continental two-door from the same stable, while James Young had a rather more individual treatment with two doors. Two years later, H.J. Mulliner produced a two-door convertible, with very similar proportions to those of the four-door saloon (and the two-door Continental as well).

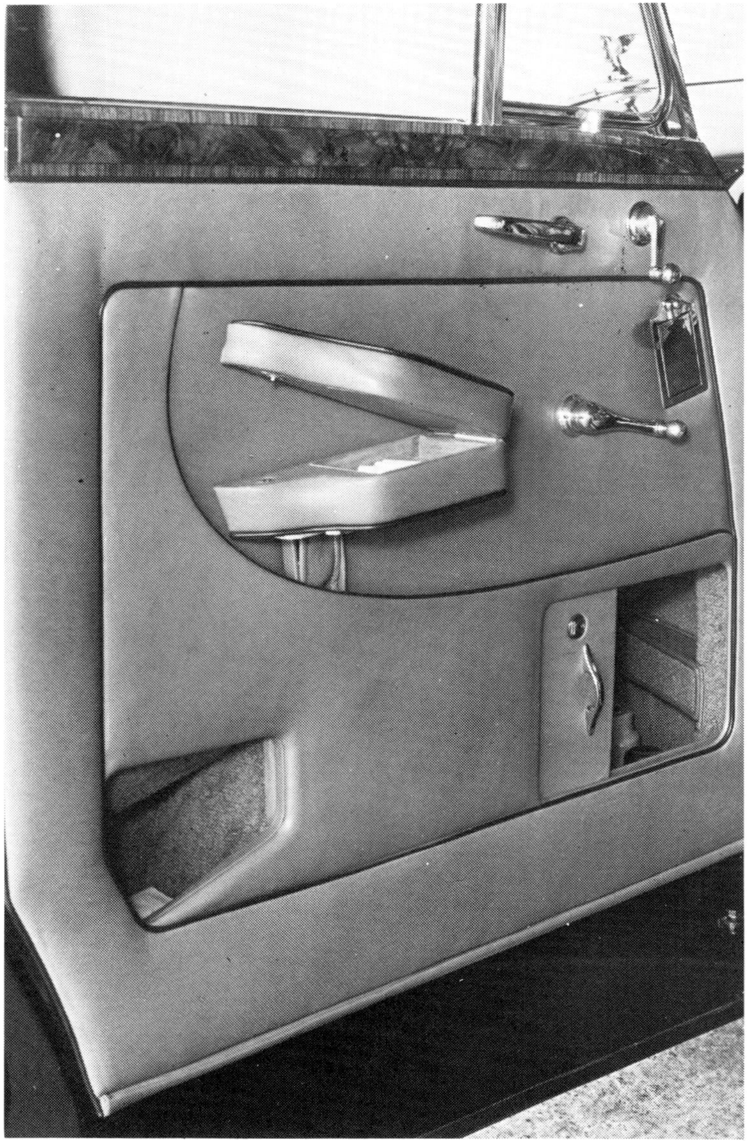

Equipment details of a James Young special body on the Bentley Mk VI in 1951, showing the way that a coachbuilder could still give his clients individual attention in this period.

Immediately after they were taken over by Rolls-Royce Ltd, H.J. Mulliner announced this attractive drophead coupe on the Silver Cloud II/S2 chassis, which was effectively a 'beheaded' version of the 'standard-steel' saloon, expensively converted to two doors . . .

. . . and in 1952, the same bodyshell was upgraded to S3 status with the four-headlamp nose.

Naturally, there was a Bentley version of the 'beheaded' H.J. Mulliner convertible of 1959 . . .

. . . which still looked very smart with the padded top erect.

The nose of a Silver Cloud III, complete with H.J. Mulliner drophead coupe bodywork. It was originally built in 1962-63.

From the rear, and even with the hood down, the H.J. Mulliner convertible looked exceptionally smart. The boot-lid badging indicates that this was one of the rare SIII Silver Cloud examples.

At this point I should mention what was effectively Freestone & Webb's final fling in this business — the amazing two-seater drophead coupe which they exhibited at Earls Court in October 1957, just before their business closed. Although it is always difficult to be certain at this end of the market, I believe this might be the only two-seater version of the Silver Cloud ever produced, and it was certainly the only one with such unique styling, which included sharp fins, concave side panels, separate bucket seats and not even a token space for a third or fourth passenger. Painted dark green, with silver flanks and a grey (power-operated) folding hood, it was a magnificent extravagance in more ways than one.

Choice became even more restricted with the arrival of the V8-engined Silver Cloud II/S2 models of October 1959, for James Young became deeply involved in the production of massive limousines on the basis of the Phantom V chassis. Henceforth, this meant that the only coachbuilder still looking after the 'standard-steel' chassis in any purposeful way was H.J. Mulliner.

In the meantime, the Chiswick-based company had itself been taken over by Rolls-Royce Ltd, who were looking to rationalize and expand their London-based coachbuilding concerns. In the meantime, however, H.J. Mulliner had been encouraged to tool-up for the production of a very smart convertible, to be built as a Rolls-Royce or a Bentley, which looked for all the world like a beheaded 'standard-steel' saloon.

This car, unveiled before the 1959 Earls Court Motor Show, was based in part on the standard pressings, but was different in many important ways. Not only was it a drophead coupe, instead of the standard saloon, but it had just two doors, instead of four. However, the front-end sheet metal, up to and including the windscreen, was standard, as was the panelling behind the line of the rear wheels and below the waist, while the sweep of the wing line was exactly the same as that of the saloons. The big door panels, like the bonnet and the boot lid, were all made from an aluminium alloy, the hood folded away or was erected completely under power operation (as an optional extra), and there were fold-down glass quarter-panels immediately behind the door glasses. That body style remained on the market for four years, until 1963, with the last cars having the four-headlamp nose and the more powerful engine of the Silver Cloud III/S3 standard models.

In 1963, however, and for the last two seasons, the lookalike drophead was discontinued, no more Bentley S3 special-coachwork cars were assembled, and the remaining Rolls-Royces — two-door saloons or two-door drophead coupes were really no more than 'badge-engineered' S-Type Bentley Continentals. As I have already pointed out in Chapter 6, the lines of the Park Ward S2 Continental, first seen as a drophead coupe in October 1959, but later offered as a coupe (or saloon — decide on a description for yourselves) with a metal roof and similar accommodation, were quite unmistakable, for this was the first ever Rolls-Royce or Bentley to be put on sale with a 'straight through' sweep of front and rear wing crown lines, from headlamp hoods to tail lamp peak. By the time the Rolls-Royce version appeared, of course, the bodies were being made by the

This smart estate car conversion on the Silver Cloud I was by Harold Radford and, with left-hand drive, was clearly destined for export.

110

Three detail views of the adaptation and equipment carried out by Harold Radford on the Silver Cloud or SI models in the mid-1950s. Rear seats could be folded forward, Grundig tape dictating equipment fitted, and extra cocktail or picnic equipment could also be added.

This graceful Rolls-Royce Silver Cloud I sports saloon by Freestone & Webb used the same basic lines as those already depicted for the earlier chassis with Bentley radiators, but with many entirely different panels.

Freestone & Webb produced this rather characterless sports saloon body for the Bentley SI towards the end of 1955. The Willesden-based company, somehow, was beginning to lose its styling touch by this time.

Freestone & Webb's final fling was at Earls Court in 1957, where their Silver Cloud bodyshell had this extraordinary rear wing/boot compartment feature.

Perhaps this was the on y two-seater bodyshell ever produced for the Rolls-Royce Silver Cloud — by Freestone & Webb in 1957. Not only did it have two seats, but it had concave flanks, two-tone paintwork and rear wing fins!

amalgamated concern of H.J. Mulliner, Park Ward.

With the all-new monocoque Silver Shadow/Bentley T-Series ready to be announced in October 1965, Rolls-Royce were quite happy to let this remaining bespoke business fade away completely in 1965 — until circumstances changed. Just as the close-down time for all Silver Cloud/S-Series production approached, it became clear that the Silver Shadow was not quite ready to be put on sale. It was neither practically nor economically possible to ask Pressed Steel to set up all their jigs and presses for another very limited run of Silver Cloud shells, so to tide themselves over the company decided to have a final burst of building special-coachbuilt Silver Cloud IIIs (and Bentley Continentals, which were virtually the same in all respects by this time).

From September to December 1965, therefore, a total of 111 Silver Cloud III rolling chassis in the CSC . . . series were produced and sent off to H.J. Mulliner, Park Ward for drophead coupe or two-door saloon coachwork of the 'straight through wing line' style to be fitted. The last chassis of all to leave Crewe was CSC 81C, on December 6, 1965 (a week after the last Continental chassis had done so), and this was the last separate-chassis Silver Cloud III to be despatched to a customer. The body style in question was a drophead coupe, and the despatch date was June 2, 1966. Production of separate chassis types, except for the Phantom V, which carried on, had therefore occupied just 20 postwar years.

After the Silver Shadow went into production, it was obviously much more difficult for special coachwork to be constructed on the basis of the monocoque bodyshell, which explains why James Young only produced 50 two-door conversions (35 Rolls-Royce, 15 Bentley), and then abandoned the project completely. H.J. Mulliner, Park Ward, being factory-owned, were in a much stronger position, and put their two-door coupe and drophead types on sale from 1966 and 1967, respectively; in 1971 these cars were re-engineered and renamed Corniche, and are with us to this day, although the name has changed yet again. But all this is for another book in this *Collector's Guide* series!

This special-bodied Rolls-Royce is actually a Silver Cloud III chassis and an H.J. Mulliner, Park Ward Flying Spur bodyshell, with the Rolls-Royce radiator. Rolls-Royce were as clever at badge engineering as anyone else.

Even though they eventually dropped out of the coachbuilding business in 1959, Hooper still managed to offer smart four-door sports saloons on the basis of the Silver Cloud in the late 1950s.

James Young offered this neat and understated two-door saloon style on the Silver Cloud and Bentley S-Series chassis in the late 1950s and early 1960s, though the details (like those bulbous headlamps!) were different on individual examples.

Typical of so many coachbuilt styles on Rolls-Royce or Bentley chassis in the 1950s was this Park Ward layout, complete with picnic tables, drop-down glass division and radio controls.

In the late 1950s, H.J. Mulliner produced this facia style on two-door or four-door Bentleys and Rolls-Royces — this left-hand-drive layout being in a Rolls-Royce.

More resourceful badge engineering — the basic bodyshell is the two-door Park Ward 'straght-through' style introduced in 1959 and built for more than six years, but this was a Rolls-Royce version on the standard Silver Cloud III chassis.

The rear quarters of the Park Ward 'straight-through' bodyshell were always like this, whether the car had a Rolls-Royce or a Bentley radiator, a drophead coupe or a saloon top.

CHAPTER 8

Long-wheelbase S-Series

The stretched 'lookalikes'

Throughout the nine-year life of the first postwar 'standard-steel' saloons, from 1946 to 1955, there had been no series-built derivatives of that basic body style, but for the second type, the Silver Cloud/S-Series cars built from 1955 onwards, Rolls-Royce Ltd had more complex plans. Not only did H.J. Mulliner produce a drophead coupe body (as described in the previous chapter), but through their Park Ward subsidiary, Rolls-Royce decided to produce a long-wheelbase version of the saloon as well. This made its bow in the autumn of 1957, and was sold, with great and growing success, until the entire range was dropped in the autumn of 1965.

At first — and casual — glance, the long-wheelbase version of the standard car looks little different. It is only on closer scrutiny, when the extra length between the wheels is noted, and an entirely different door/window/floor relationship is spotted, that the extent of the change becomes clear. It is for that reason that I have elected to describe these cars in this volume about coachbuilt Rolls-Royces, rather than among the 'standard-steel' saloons.

As I have already made clear, the 'Bentley 9' chassis design of the early 1950s was always meant to be produced in a variety of wheelbase lengths, just as its predecessor had been. The standard car was to roll on a 10ft 3in wheelbase, and the planned Phantom V was to have a 12ft 1in wheelbase. There was also a third derivative, to form the basis for the long-wheelbase version of the standard saloons, to be 4 inches longer at 10ft 7in. I believe that it was no more than coincidence that this dimension was the same as that of the original Silver Wraith, for there was never any intention to use similar bodies from that earlier period, and

by the time the 'long' Silver Cloud appeared, the Silver Wraith wheelbase had been increased to 11ft 1in.

The marketing intention behind the creation of the long-wheelbase car was that it should bridge a gap between the 'standard-steel' saloon and the Silver Wraith/Phantom V, the owner-driven saloon and the chauffeur-driven limousine, the standard saloon and the special creation. Primarily, the wheelbase increase allowed a division to be fitted between front and rear seats and, as *The Autocar* commented in its description: 'The intention is that the businessman should be chauffeur-driven to and from appointments during the week, but should use the car as a normal family saloon at weekends and holiday times.' To which I would comment that their idea of a 'normal family saloon' differed completely from that of the majority of readers!

As far as the chassis was concerned, it was almost identical with that of the 'standard-steel' type, except for the extra 4 inches in the wheelbase, and when changes were made to one type, they were also made to the other. Visually, the front and rear of the two cars were identical, all the differences being accommodated between the wheels.

The extra wheelbase length had been used to allow for the division to be standardized, and for there to be a little extra space in the rear compartment, for there was no more luggage accommodation and — if anything — rather less space in the front seats. As with many cars which had a division, the front seat was a full-width bench, to which there was no fore-and-aft adjustment and where the back rest angle was fixed. The division was an integral part of the front seat structure, and the single-

In 1957, Rolls-Royce announced the long-wheelbase touring limousine Silver Cloud, with a 'standard-steel' bodyshell considerably modified by Park Ward. Note the much longer rear doors and the extra rear quarter-windows behind them.

pane screen between front and rear could be retracted downwards by electrical means. As one might expect, there were fold-down picnic tables and other fittings built in to the division structure itself.

The touring limousine bodyshell was produced by Park Ward, in North-West London, where final assembly of the cars also took place, on the basis of a 'standard-steel' shell provided by Pressed Steel. In crude terms, when Park Ward received this shell, they literally sawed it in half, behind the line of the front door, moved the two sections 4 inches apart, and began to construct a much modified structure, which still managed to look uncannily like that of the standard car.

Specifically, from the nose to the rear of the front doors, the panels and the styling lines were identical, as they were from the extreme tail forward to the line of the rear wheels and to the rear wing/rear door shut face. However, between these two points there were major differences.

Naturally, the roof panel and the floor panel were lengthened. However, there were new rear doors and frames, *and* a rear quarter-window in the limousine, which the standard car did not have. The standard car had relatively narrow drop glasses, with a fixed pane behind them, whereas on the limousine, not only was the door longer front to rear, but there was one large,

uninterrupted pane of glass above the waist. The upper glass line sweep, and the smoothly tapering waistline profile, were carried through to the new rear quarter-window, which reached further back (relatively speaking) than the rear of the glass in the standard saloon. The rear doors and the modified rear wings were skilfully shaped to blend well with the otherwise unaltered front and rear profiles.

Relative to the line of the rear wheels, the position of the rear seat was virtually unchanged, and one easy way to tell the two cars apart was that the long-wheelbase limousine had a much smaller glassless blind spot in the quarters. Usually the limousine was treated to two-tone paintwork, and it was a tribute to the care which had gone into the conversion that it looked even more handsome than before and there were no telltale compromises to give the game away.

The penalty of providing this extra space, and the limousine features, was not only in the length and the weight (increased by about 4 inches and 170lb, respectively), but in the cost of it all. When the car was introduced, in time for the Earls Court Motor Show of October 1957, the comparison of total prices was as follows:

Rolls-Royce Silver Cloud saloon £5,694
long-wheelbase limousine £6,894

The long-wheelbase Silver Cloud I looked exactly the same as the normal 'standard-steel' saloon from this view, though the presence of a chauffeur might indicate that a division is fitted.

| Bentley S-Series | saloon | £5,544 |
| | long-wheelbase limousine | £6,894 |

— to the irreverent, therefore, the equation was £300 an inch. Incidentally, it was worth noting that although there was still a premium for the Rolls-Royce radiator on the saloon, there was none on the limousine.

Now for the complications! Not only could a customer order a long-wheelbase limousine — via Park Ward — from Rolls-Royce Ltd, but if he insisted, he could have it without the division, and with the normal saloon's front seats. In addition, if he was feeling really self-indulgent, he could merely order the long-wheelbase chassis instead, and have an extra-special body style built on to it — saloon, drophead coupe or limousine — by one of the remaining independent coachbuilders. At the 1957 Motor Show, by the way, Rolls-Royce had obviously moved very fast to supply long-wheelbase chassis to these coachbuilders, well before production of Park Ward types could begin. Apart from the standard limousine on the Park Ward stand, there was a four-

The long-wheelbase Silver Cloud, with 'standard-steel' saloon body modified to touring limousine form by Park Ward, had much more space in the rear passenger compartment, but the same boot as usual. There was also a Bentley derivative of this bodyshell.

The long-wheelbase touring limousine, by Park Ward out of 'standard-steel' saloon, became more and more popular over the years. This was the SIII version, built between 1962 and 1965.

door/six-window saloon by Freestone & Webb, a four-door saloon by Hooper and a four-door touring limousine by James Young. A feature of the Freestone & Webb style was that the wings of the car were entirely separated from the boot compartment by a deep fore-and-aft recess with sharp edges.

[It was at this show, incidentally, that F & W also showed that amazing two-seater Silver Cloud 'sports car', complete with concave sides, and a two-tone paint job. Was it just coincidence that the business closed down within a year . . . ?]

Production and sales of the long-wheelbase cars got under way relatively slowly at first, but built up steadily in the months and years to come. In the first two years, from autumn 1957 to autumn 1959, when all the cars were powered by the 4.9-litre six-cylinder engine, a total of 121 Silver Cloud and 35 S-Series cars were built, which averages out at about six chassis a month. The very first long-wheelbase chassis was despatched from Crewe to a coachbuilder in June 1957, but the first 'standard shape' deliveries began in September, immediately after announcement, and the first Bentley-radiatored type left in November. Demand for Bentley, as opposed to Rolls-Royce, derivatives was always limited, no doubt because there was no price differential between the two badges on this car; the ratio fell from one in five (S1) to one in 10 (S3).

It is fascinating to see that, at this level, there was no reluctance to 'gild the lily' with a special bodyshell, even though the extra cost was considerable. Consider, for instance, that at a time when the 'standard-steel' Silver Cloud cost £5,694 and a standard long-wheelbase limousine cost £6,984, there was still significant demand for — say — a James Young saloon at £7,629, or even a Mulliner drophead coupe at £8,326. By mid-1980s money, therefore, one had to pay an extra £8,000 to £10,000 for the privilege of getting a special coachbuilt style.

By this time, in fact, Rolls-Royce had begun to arrange discreet deals with their favoured coachbuilders, so that not all of them tried to cater for all models and all types of business. As far as the long-wheelbase cars were concerned, Rolls-Royce made sure that Park Ward only produced the standard-shape

An early version of the long-wheelbase Park Ward touring limousine rear compartment, with hand-winding windows.

Unlike the car illustrated on the previous page, this touring limousine (an SII, in fact) features electric window operation, and has an ashtray built into the furniture of the division.

The facia and instrument layout of the Park Ward-built Silver Cloud long-wheelbase limousine. The car has a bench-type front seat, the automatic transmission quadrant is on the right of the steering column, and the pull-and-twist handbrake grip is near the front door pillar.

Two views of the H.J. Mulliner four-door cabriolet body style specially developed for the long-wheelbase (10ft 7in) Silver Cloud II chassis. Although the family resemblance to both the current Bentley Continental and the Flying Spur bodies is obvious, and there are some common panels, quite a bit of unique coachbuilding was needed in this case.

machines (while building several hundred Alvis saloon and drophead coupe shells as well, starting in 1958); for first-series chassis, James Young produced 22 special styles (five of them Bentleys) and Hooper 20 cars (seven of them Bentleys), with only two coming from Freestone & Webb and two from H.J. Mulliner, all of them really being 'motor show specials', not committed even to limited production.

When the V8 engine was introduced in the autumn of 1959, and the cars respectively became Silver Cloud II and S2, the long-wheelbase cars were updated in parallel. As with the standard cars, demand perked up significantly, and in the next three years an average of 10 cars a month were built, the first (LSPA4) leaving in August 1959 for the USA and the last (SAE673) being delivered to a UK customer in October 1962.

With the second-series cars, the trend to fewer special coachbuilt examples continued. In three years, only 41 Rolls-Royce and a mere six Bentley 'specials' were built. Interestingly enough, almost all of them (43 in all, only five of which were Bentleys) came from the James Young workshops at Bromley, in Kent, where they kept very good company with the Phantom V limousines and saloons for which that concern was noted. By this time, of course, Freestone & Webb and Hooper had gone out of the coachbuilding business, while H.J. Mulliner was committed to lookalike drophead coupe production, and gradual integration with Park Ward.

Finally, from 1962, came the Silver Cloud III and S3 long-wheelbase cars, built at the slightly slower rate of eight cars a month, though there were a few more special coachbuilt examples than with the second-series machines. All cars, whether standard style or coachbuilt, were fitted with four headlamps, and the special coachbuilt styles now had much panelwork in common with that provided for the normal-wheelbase Bentley Continental chassis. A grand total of 285 third-series/four-headlamp machines were eventually produced, of which 54 had special body styles (49 of them from James Young, the other five all being from H.J. Mulliner, Park Ward as something of a final flourish).

By most standards, therefore, the long-wheelbase programme of 1957 to 1965 was a success, with a total of 797 cars of all types eventually being built. There was no attempt to extend the life of these cars beyond the span of the 'standard-steel' saloons, for the last long-wheelbase Bentley S3 left Park Ward on September 3, 1965, and the last Silver Cloud III (James Young-bodied) on October 1, 1965, just before the monocoque Silver Shadow was revealed.

For a latter-day collector, of course, the long-wheelbase models, in their standard style, are quite feasible cars to buy for restoration, as much of the bodyshell is the same, or nearly the same, as that of a 'standard-steel' saloon. With the special coachbuilt long-wheelbase cars, of which there were 149, the body situation is, of course, desperate, as it is with all such machines where the coachbuilders have either gone out of business (like James Young) or not preserved many spare body panels (like all surviving coachbuilders). The restoration of such cars, after all, is part of the pride — and the anguish — of owning a 'classic' Rolls-Royce or Bentley.

CHAPTER 9

H.J. Mulliner and Park Ward

The 'in-house' coachbuilders

Early in 1984, the Rolls-Royce Motors magazine *Journal* recorded the news that: 'the massive reorganization and relocation of the Mulliner Park Ward Division at Hythe Road has been completed on schedule'. In the mid-1980s, work at Hythe Road, Willesden, London NW10, is concentrated on the Corniche and Phantom VI models, but at one time Park Ward was in that part of London on its own, H.J. Mulliner was in Chiswick, several miles away, and both concerns were independent. It was not until the end of the 1950s that both had been drawn into the Rolls-Royce organization. Along the way, there had been fascinating and complex events.

Like many great British coachbuilders, H.J. Mulliner can trace their existence back over many years. In the beginning, Henry Jervis Mulliner's father founded a business in Liverpool in 1854, but by the end of the century, not only was a small company called Mulliner London Ltd in operation, along with H.J. Mulliner & Co, but there was also Arthur Mulliner of Northampton, and Mulliners of Birmingham, all branches of the same family and all in the same line of business.

H.J. Mulliner himself retired from his business in 1908, two years after the company had outgrown its Brook Street address and moved to new premises at Bath Road, Bedford Park, Chiswick, the new owners being John Croall and Sons, of Edinburgh. 'H.J.' was a close friend of the Hon C.S. Rolls from the early days of the Rolls-Royce concern's foundation, and his business expanded rapidly. After a busy First World War, the company enlarged the Chiswick premises, still building bodywork on a variety of chassis, though with a steadily increasing emphasis on Rolls-Royce and the still-independent Bentley concern.

Early in the 1920s, H.J. Mulliner took up Weymann body construction, and were reputedly the first to apply such technology to a Rolls-Royce chassis; they were also the first specialist concern to start using cellulose paint. By the 1930s, H.J. Mulliner were building almost exclusively for Rolls-Royce Ltd (who had absorbed Bentley at the end of 1931), and after the Second World War (which included building contracts for Mosquito and Hamilcar aircraft), the company found its services even more in demand. Apart from making a batch of Humber Pullman sedanca de ville bodies for Rootes in the 1940s, the company devoted itself exclusively to the clothing of Rolls-Royce and Bentley products, and to make sure they could always do this they took over additional premises in Fulham.

I have already mentioned some of the most important contracts carried out by H.J. Mulliner in the postwar period, but it bears repeating that the very first Rolls-Royce production chassis (WTA1, a 1946 Silver Wraith) went to H.J. Mulliner for its bodyshell and was subsequently used by Rolls-Royce management, that the original Phantom IV, for H.R.H. Princess Elizabeth, was bodied by H.J. Mulliner, and that the styling of the Silver Cloud/S-Series cars was strongly influenced by the H.J. Mulliner 'lightweight' model produced on Mk VI Bentleys in the early 1950s.

As I have already mentioned, the original R-Type Bentley Continental was a product of the co-operation between Ivan Evernden, from Crewe, and H.J. Mulliner's then Technical Director, Stanley Watts, and the first of the Flying Spur four-door cars on the Bentley Continental S1 chassis also had the

A mixed bag, to show that Park Ward built Alvis TD21 bodies in the same factory as they produced special coachwork for Rolls-Royce and Bentley cars. The year is 1959, and a line of Rolls-Royce shells is in the background.

same coachbuilder's bodywork.

Even as early as 1950, H.J. Mulliner had started to investigate alternatives to seasoned wood for their body skeletons, eventually choosing to use extruded alloy sections under the sleek skins, progressively from the arrival of the R-Type Continental. It was no wonder that H.J. Mulliner, its Managing Director, Arthur Johnstone, and the entire staff, continued to draw ever closer to Rolls-Royce Ltd, even though that firm already had a bodybuilding subsidiary at Park Ward, in Willesden. At the beginning of the 1950s, and well into that decade, H.J. Mulliner would still have up to four different bodies in limited series production; 1957, for instance, saw the display at Earls Court of a four-door Bentley Flying Spur, a two-door coupe Continental, a Silver Cloud convertible and a Silver Wraith touring limousine.

The numbers, too, were impressive, for H.J. Mulliner produced 193 of the 208 R-Type Continentals, more S-Type Continentals than any other concern, and had the lion's share of coachbuilt business for the Mk VI and R-Type Bentleys and the Rolls-Royce Silver Wraith.

All the time, however, trading conditions were becoming progressively more difficult, for the number of people demanding bespoke coachwork fell steadily and depressingly throughout the 1950s, partly, I am sure, because of the excellence achieved by Rolls-Royce on their own 'standard-steel' bodywork. The solution, in the end, was for H.J. Mulliner and Co Ltd to be bought by Rolls-Royce Ltd, and for the new parent company to organize future business on more streamlined lines.

The occasion for this, of course, was the decision to build a modern drophead coupe body style in significant numbers on the Silver Cloud II/Bentley S2 chassis. This car, which kept the same wing lines and front end as the standard car, was a

When Freestone & Webb was at its peak, in the mid-1950s, the workshops looked like this. An all-wood skeleton for a big Rolls-Royce limousine is being put together in the background, and hanging from the ceiling are literally hundreds of formers for roof, bonnet and wing profiles of the coachbuilt cars.

lightweight two-door car and needed a lot of preparation. Well before it was ready for release, in the summer of 1959, therefore, H.J. Mulliner was taken over.

By this time, Park Ward and Co Ltd had already been a wholly-owned subsidiary of Rolls-Royce for 20 years; although by H.J. Mulliner's standards, the Park Ward enterprise was very young indeed, it was swept into the Rolls-Royce 'empire' as early as 1939.

In fact, Park Ward was founded in 1919 when W.M. Park and C.W. Ward got together in Willesden, with financial assistance from Granville Bradshaw, and soon developed a reputation for offering really stylish coachwork on a variety of chassis. Like H.J. Mulliner, however, Park Ward came to concentrate on producing bodywork for Rolls-Royce and Bentley cars in the 1930s.

In the 1930s, too, Park Ward took a real step forward by

patenting a new type of bodyshell construction, where the wooden frame was displaced by steel pressings or small castings. It meant that the weight of their bodyshells was reduced significantly, while being even more rigid than before, and it also meant that rot, in the long term, might be reduced.

By the late 1930s, Park Ward was still independent, still growing, but getting very close to Rolls-Royce, who would commission batches of up to 25 standardized styles at a time, then make sure their customers were steered in the direction of London NW10! A Park Ward body style, like a Gurney Nutting style, became instantly recognizable by its rakish lines.

The mini-recession of 1937-38, however, hit the independent coachbuilding industry quite hard, one immediate result being that Barker were taken over by Hooper, and another was that several other firms became frightened about their future prospects. Providentially for Park Ward, the new Rolls-Royce

The Park Ward full-size drawing-board, circa 1950, with a new sports saloon style taking shape. The model says 'RR 1945' on its number-plate, and it looks years out of date!

'standardization plan' had already been agreed in principle by this time, and with a view to protecting its sources of bodies, Rolls-Royce made a bid for Park Ward in 1939, which was instantly accepted.

In the postwar years, Park Ward progressively became an integrated part of the Rolls-Royce empire, not only by taking on approved coachbuilding work, but also by tackling a lot of prototype fabrication for the parent concern. The first prototype bodyshells for the Bentley Mk VI and the Rolls-Royce Silver Cloud ('Bentley 9', as it was coded at the time), were built at Park Ward.

Until the 1960s, however, the Park Ward business had more capacity than Rolls-Royce activity, and it was to rectify this — to keep the workforce fully employed — that Rolls-Royce encouraged Park Ward to go out and bid, successfully, for the contract to supply Alvis with saloon and drophead coupe bodies for the TD21 3-litre chassis. This was a very successful enterprise, for between 1958 and 1967 Park Ward built well over 1,500 such shells for Alvis; in the end, the contract was not lost, but really faded out, as Alvis gradually withdrew from the private car market. Thereafter, the coachbuilding business concentrated solely on Rolls-Royce's needs.

Statistics show that Park Ward and H.J. Mulliner shared most of the business in building bodies for the more sporty, high-performance cars from Crewe, though H.J. Mulliner and James Young (not forgetting Freestone & Webb until 1957) seemed to have an edge where dignified limousines were concerned. Even so, Park Ward did a lot of work on the Silver Wraith in all its forms, found a ready market for their two types of S-Series Bentley Continentals and — from 1957 — were responsible for producing the long-wheelbase limousines as a conversion of 'standard-steel' Rolls-Royce Silver Cloud and S-Series Bentley bodies. That contract alone accounted for the erection of 648 shells, for which demand was just as high in the mid-1960s as it had been in the beginning.

By 1960, therefore, Rolls-Royce controlled the destinies of

By 1950, Park Ward had completely abandoned structural wood for its bodyshells, as this part-built car makes clear.

The arrival of the monocoque Silver Shadow/T-Series finally killed off James Young's hopes of staying in business. They built 50 of these two-door cars (some Bentley-radiatored like this, some Rolls-Royce), but found the process prohibitively expensive.

two separate coachbuilders, H.J. Mulliner producing a mixture of 'traditional' and all-metal bodies, while Park Ward concentrated on long-wheelbase conversions, and used their patented type of all-metal bodywork for cars as diverse as the S-Series Continental convertibles and the Phantom V limousines. It was becoming noticeable, however, that major styling changes were not being made as often as in the past, for the use of all-metal coachwork, with a modicum of stretcher-press/Kirksite tooling, meant that production runs had to be longer to justify the investment. In any case, cars like the convertible Silver Cloud/S-Series (H.J. Mulliner) and the long-wheelbase limousine Silver Clouds (Park Ward), were based on standard coachwork styles, which themselves had a long life.

Clearly, therefore, it made economic sense to bring the two 'in-house' coachbuilding concerns closer together, financially, commercially and — eventually — geographically. Accordingly, in 1961, a new company called H.J. Mulliner, Park Ward Ltd had been set up, with headquarters at the long-established Park Ward factory in High Road, Willesden, London NW10. In due course, the old H.J. Mulliner factory in Bedford Park, Chiswick, about three miles south of Park Ward, was closed down and sold off.

Even by 1963, the rationalization had become obvious, for M-P-W's Earls Court Motor Show offerings, all on one stand, included such 'cocktails' as a Rolls-Royce version of the Park Ward 'straight-through' Bentley Continental convertible — but built as a two-door saloon — and a four-door Rolls-Royce, which was also a modified Bentley Flying Spur, this originally being an H.J. Mulliner style! The huge but dignified Park Ward Phantom V limousine was only slightly changed (the four-headlamp style had been adopted a year earlier) but it was now officially placarded as having coachwork by 'H.J. Mulliner, Park Ward'.

Until the end of Silver Cloud/S-Series production, the coachbuilding subsidiary carried on in the time-honoured fashion. Continentals, Phantom Vs, or long-wheelbase lookalike limousines would all take shape at Crewe, up to the completed rolling chassis stage, in which state they were capable of being driven to check out all the systems. These chassis, whether of 10ft 3in, 10ft 7in, or 12ft 1in wheelbase length, would then be sent down to London by car transporter, where body construction would proceed.

In the heyday of individual styling, six months might elapse between the arrival of the chassis at High Road and the delivery of the complete car to the customer, but by the early 1960s, when standardization was far advanced, the delay had been cut to two or three months in most cases. Bodyshells for the long-wheelbase limousines and the 'standard style' Bentley Continentals could, in any case, be built up on jigs and slave chassis before their own individual chassis arrived at High Road. The long-wheelbase limousine shells started life as complete 'standard-steel' bodies, delivered direct and unpainted from the Pressed Steel Company at Cowley, less than 50 miles away.

Not only were bodyshells built at Mulliner, Park Ward, but the cars were completely finished off — which means that they were painted, trimmed, wired, furnished, checked out and road-tested — before delivery to the customer. Only in very special cases was it necessary to return a coachbuilt car to the Rolls-Royce factory at Crewe for further attention.

Phantom V and Phantom VI limousine and landaulette production, of course, always took longer than for the other cars. It was quite usual for a Phantom V or VI to be 'in the works' for up to six months, and a landaulette for much longer. However, even the limousine bodyshell had no wood in its framework, steel and light-alloy panelling being used throughout. There was simple jigging for bodyshell construction, something which prewar craftsmen would not have expected, or needed, but has been well-justified in this case for a body style that has been produced for more than 25 years.

Postscript

Apart from continued production of Phantom V and Phantom VI limousines, all assembly of separate-chassis Rolls-Royce and Bentley models came to an end in 1966 as the monocoque Silver Shadow/T-Series cars began to appear. Accordingly, limousine assembly was shunted into a corner, and Mulliner, Park Ward was completely (and expensively) converted to produce special versions of that body. The two-door saloon, with graceful 'coke-bottle' wing line, was introduced in the spring of 1966, and the drophead coupe version followed in the autumn of 1967, both using the underpan, running gear and some inner panels of the new Silver Shadow. From 1971, these cars were renamed Corniche, and in 1975 they were joined by a Pininfarina-styled two-door coupe, the Rolls-Royce Camargue. At the time of writing, not only the Corniche and the Camargue, but the Phantom VI, are still with us, though during the 1970s the majority of H.J. Mulliner, Park Ward production was moved the short distance from High Road, to Hythe Road, NW10 (previously Rolls-Royce's London service station). The old Park Ward factory at High Road was abandoned and it no longer exists, for not long ago it was knocked down and redeveloped.

CHAPTER 10

Restoring a coachbuilt car

Anyone setting out to revive a coachbuilt Rolls-Royce or Bentley to its former glory has my heartfelt sympathy. It is not merely that it will take a great deal of time and money (nothing comes cheaply where a Rolls-Royce is concerned), but that it will require so much personal research and individual enterprise.

If you can discount the expense, the restoration of a historic Jaguar, MG, or Cadillac is relatively straightforward, for there are not only many other examples of particular models on the road, but the supply of parts, even body panels, is often good.With a Rolls-Royce or Bentley of the type we have been considering in this volume, the situation is not at all as encouraging.

It is one thing to tackle the rejuvenation of the chassis and running gear of — say — a Bentley Continental or a Silver Wraith, but it is quite another to deal with the bodywork. The problem is two-fold — almost all the once-famous coachbuilding concerns have now closed down, and new spare body panels for such limited-production bodyshells were never in abundance, even while the cars were in current production.

First of all I should list the current (1984) status of the major coachbuilding concerns mentioned in this book:

H.J. Mulliner — Taken over by Rolls-Royce in 1959, merged with Park Ward in 1961, no longer operating as a separate business.

Park Ward — Merged with H.J. Mulliner in 1961, no longer operating as a separate business, and has concentrated on monocoque production since 1966.

James Young — Withdrew from the coachbuilding business in 1967, soon after the Silver Shadow/T-Series came on to the market, at which point they built the last of their graceful Phantom Vs. Had been owned by the Jack Barclay Group for some years.

Freestone & Webb — Taken over by the Swain Group in May 1957, Freestone & Webb showed some extraordinary styles later that year, then went out of business. By 1958, no trace was left.

Hooper — Owned by the Daimler concern since the late 1930s, Hooper stopped making coachbuilt bodies in 1959. The name lives on, but none of the old records or drawings survive in the new company's hands, as they are in the hands of the Science Museum.

Harold Radford — After the mid-1950s, this company concentrated on the conversion of 'standard-steel' shells, rather than on new construction, and later changed to making special Mini-Coopers and other conversions.

Many other notable concerns, such as Abbott, Graber, Vanden Plas, Gurney Nutting and Franay, occasionally built special bodies on Rolls-Royce or Bentley postwar chassis, but all have been out of business for years, and no records survived.

The situation, therefore, regarding the restoring of coachbuilt bodyshells for these cars is desperate, for unless I have overlooked some rare and exotic cache of material, it seems that neither parts nor drawings for these exist any more. The only cars for which panels exist today are:

Phantom V and Phantom VI: Since the Phantom VI is still in very limited production, it follows that the jigs and formers are still in use at H.J. Mulliner, Park Ward. Except for the fact that current cars have a four-headlamp nose, and the 1959-62 Phantom Vs had a two-headlamp nose, there are many common

A restoration might have to include the complete reconstruction of wooden body framing, as typified by this mid-1950s Silver Wraith limousine — and no spare parts will be available!

There will be no new spare body panels for a coachbuilt car, so panels will have to be made up by hand, by experts. Originally these were produced using wheeling machines, and they required a great deal of expertise.

panels used to this day. As to the costs, well . . .

This advice, of course, does not apply to James Young-bodied Phantom Vs.

'Beheaded' two-door H.J. Mulliner convertibles: Built between 1959 and 1963, this style used standard sheet metal up to the windscreen, and some standard sheet metal around the tail. In addition, the wing profile along the flanks was the same as for the standard saloons, though it was, of course, a two-door conversion. Since Silver Cloud panels are still available, it follows that with a great deal of resource this 'beheaded' convertible can be rebuilt.

Long-wheelbase Park Ward limousine, 1957-1965: This body was largely based on that of the 'standard-steel' saloon, though much of the centre of the shell and the rear quarters, not forgetting the division, was unique. In many cases, however, standard parts will be useful for rebuilding a long-wheelbase car.

My advice for all would-be restorers of coachbuilt Rolls-Royces and Bentleys, however, would be first of all to make sure that you have a genuine and original machine, then investigate the slimmest of chances that some parts might be obtainable,

The building of a coachbuilt style needed hundreds of hours of careful panel work, and restoration will be no less easy. This was a Hooper scene in 1957.

next locate a well-qualified restoration specialist — and finally make sure that you have a *lot* more money than you originally estimate will be necessary! (There are always delays, hidden horrors to be exposed and other complications.)

The question of originality is important, not only because that will eventually underpin the value of the restored car, but because it may clear up all manner of puzzles found during restoration. There is not only the possibility of a Bentley having been 'converted' to a Rolls-Royce (something which is easy enough to detect, unless the various chassis, body and engine numbers have been switched, and details like the pedals and the instrument markings have also been changed), but one body might have been 'married' to another chassis. Don't worry — I am not giving away any trade secrets, for it has all been seen in the past. The Rolls-Royce Enthusiasts' Club regularly get enquiries asking for certain details to be checked against the original chassis and record cards which they hold.

There is no doubt that any historic Rolls-Royce or Bentley owner of the period I cover in this book should be in the Enthusiasts' Club, who are found at: The Rolls-Royce Enthusiasts' Club, The Hunt House, Paulerspury, Northamptonshire. Tel: 032 733 788. (Hon. Secretary: Lt.Col. E.B. Barrass).

Although all post-1931 Bentley records are held by the RREC, there are many good reasons, too, for joining the Bentley Drivers Club, especially if a Bentley owner has sporting pretentions. Their headquarters are at: Bentley Drivers Club, 16 Clearley Road, Long Crendon, Aylesbury, Bucks. Tel: 0844-208233. (Secretary: Mrs B.M. Fell).

Although I am sure it is unwise to quote actual values, or asking prices for the various models (after all, these vary widely from country to country, even from year to year), it is possible to put some sort of pecking order on values as I see them in the mid-1980s:

The rarest of all are the Phantom IVs, a few of which have been broken up, and some which are still with their original owners. If one became available, it would be wise to pay the asking price and slip discreetly away — if, that is, you are determined to have such a car.

R-Type Continentals are relatively rare, and much sought

after due to their styling and performance. However, they are not *that* rare, as Stanley Sedgwick's 1970s research proved, and all but a handful have the same H.J. Mulliner two-door fastback styling.

Truly distinctive coachbuilt cars, like the 'beheaded' drophead coupes of the early 1960s and the Rolls-Royce version of the Park Ward 'straight through' style based on the Continental, are also rare and valuable, but cars like the Bentley Flying Spur, the long-wheelbase 'standard-steel'-shape limousines and any number of Silver Wraiths, are relatively common.

So, too, are Phantom V limousines, though many of these are still in use for civic and company duties and rarely come on to the market. In any case, is a Phantom V or VI *really* the sort of car many people restore and take to concours events in the mid-1980s?

Perhaps, too, at this juncture I should emphasize that a Bentley was just as well-designed and well-built as a Rolls-Royce of the same period, for their running gear was virtually identical in many instances, and special coachwork styles were built by the same team of skilled craftsmen, in the same departments, often on the same jigs. None of which, of course, will ever convince some people, whose opinion is that the Rolls-Royce is automatically the best . . .

As I have made clear in the companion volume to this work, Appleyard Rippon Ltd, of Leeds, hold the worldwide franchise to supply parts for the cars of the 1945 to 1965 period, although Rolls-Royce Motors continue to manufacture new spares from time to time, as and when the demand justifies this. Always remembering that the car's chassis number and engine number should be known and quoted, it is encouraging just how many mechanical parts can still be found for these cars.

Unhappily, though, the only way to ensure the rebuilding of a bodyshell, especially one of the very individual, handbuilt, styles found on cars like the Silver Wraith, is to have it done by a specialist. Membership of one or other of the one-make clubs at least ensures that their best advice is available. Different firms,

Careful rubbing down before filling, then painting this door Similar work will need to be done all over again on an old Rolls-Royce or Bentley, as no new panels for special-coachwork types still exist.

in different countries, have established a reputation, and in spite of the fact that they will be expensive, their work is to be recommended. At least it is a comfort to know that a Silver Wraith can as easily be repaired or reconstructed in California, Australia or South Africa as it can in Great Britain.

More than half of all Rolls-Royces ever built are still on the road, it is said, and the proportion is surely even higher for the cars considered in this book. If you have ever had the pleasure of driving, or merely inspecting, one of them, you will know why this should be so. The Best Car in the World is always worth preserving.

APPENDIX A

Technical specifications

As I have made clear in the text, and in the companion volume to this book which deals with the 'standard-steel' Rolls-Royce and Bentley models, the whole range of models produced between 1946 and 1965 was based on only two fundamentally different chassis layouts. In the case of the coachbuilt models, of course, the second of these layouts persists to this day. No matter what the marque badge, engine size and coachwork fitted, only one of two chassis types would be found under the glossy skin.

From 1946 to 1959, the original postwar chassis, suspension, engine and transmission types was used as the basis for building the Silver Wraith, Phantom IV and Bentley R-Type Continental; this, of course, was the chassis used under the Bentley Mk VI and R-Type and the Rolls-Royce Silver Dawn 'standard-steel' saloons.

The second-generation chassis type, first seen under the 'standard-steel' Rolls-Royce Silver Cloud and Bentley S1 models of 1955, has been used on every separate-chassis/coachbuilt Bentley or Rolls-Royce built since 1959. This embraces the S-Type Continental Bentleys, Flying Spurs and their relatives, the Rolls-Royce Phantom V and Phantom VI and other cars with coachbuilt shells. At the time of writing, a handful of Phantom VI cars are still being built each year, but the chassis has been around for nearly 30 years, and production may well draw to a close very soon. I do not expect it to survive 1985.

Clearly, as special and individual coachwork was mounted on many of these chassis, it has not always been possible to give accurate weights and bodyshell dimensions. However, where possible, these are made clear.

Rolls-Royce Silver Wraith — produced 1946 to 1959
Original specification:
Engine: 6-cyl, overhead inlet, side exhaust valves, 88.9 × 114.3mm, 4,257cc (3.5 × 4.5in, 259.9cu in), CR 6.4:1. Single dual-choke downdraught Stromberg carburettor. Peak power never officially revealed, estimated at approximately 120-125bhp (net) at 3,750rpm.
Transmission: 11in single-dry-plate clutch, with centrifugal assistance, and 4-speed manual gearbox, with no synchromesh on first gear. Rear axle ratio 3.727:1. Overall gear ratios 3.727, 5.001, 7.520, 11.113, reverse 11.767:1.
Suspension and brakes: Ifs, coil springs, wishbones, anti-roll bar

and lever-arm hydraulic dampers; live rear axle, half-elliptic leaf springs and adjustable (by driver's lever control) lever-arm hydraulic dampers. Cam-and-roller steering, 3.5 turns lock-to-lock. 12.25 × 2.6in diameter front and rear brakes with mechanical servo assistance (servo mounted on transmission). Choice of 7.00-16in cross-ply tyres on 5in steel disc wheels, or 6.50-17in cross-ply tyres on 5in steel disc wheels.
Dimensions: Wheelbase 10ft 7in (322.6cm); front track 4ft 10.5in (148.6cm); rear track 5ft 0in (152.4cm). Depending on choice of coachwork, overall length about 17ft 2in (523cm); width 6ft 0in (183cm); height 5ft 10in (178cm). Unladen weight, approx 4,700lb. (2,132kg).
Basic price when introduced in 1946: £2,035 for rolling chassis to coachbuilder, £3,325 to £3,675 for complete coachbuilt car, depending on body and fittings.
Development changes: The Silver Wraith chassis not only benefited from changes progressively introduced to other 'standard-steel' Bentley and Rolls-Royce saloons, but was also given updating modifications of its own. These included: 4,566cc (278.6cu in) engine fitted from mid-1951, soon with single-choke Zenith carb. 4,566cc engine with higher (6.75:1) compression for some markets from mid-1952. 4,887cc (298cu in) engine fitted from mid/late 1954. 4,887cc engine fitted with twin SU carburettors from mid-1956 and larger SUs from late 1956. RR-General Motors Hydramatic four-speed automatic transmission became optional on cars delivered from late 1952. An optional 3.417:1 final-drive ratio was available on most series and, from 1955, a Silver Cloud-type 3.89:1 ratio was also made available. From mid-1951 (first complete car deliveries from January 1952) the wheelbase was increased and, henceforth, all major dimensions were as follows: Wheelbase 11ft 1in (337.8cm); front track 4ft 10.5in (148.6cm); rear track 5ft 4in (162.6cm). Depending on coachwork chosen, overall length about 17ft 4in (528cm). Unladen weight up to 5,200lb (2,358kg). Basic prices in autumn 1951 were: £2,195 for rolling chassis to coachbuilder and about £4,340 for complete coachbuilt car, depending on body and fittings.

Rolls-Royce Phantom IV — produced 1950 to 1956
Engine: 8-cyl, overhead inlet, side exhaust valves, 88.9 × 114.3mm, 5,675cc (3.5 × 4.5in, 346.5cu in), CR 6.4:1. Single downdraught dual-choke Stromberg carburettor. Peak power never officially revealed, estimated at approx 170bhp (nett) at 3,800rpm.
Transmission: 11in single-dry-plate clutch, with synchromesh assistance, and 4-speed manual gearbox, with no synchromesh on first gear. Final-drive ratio 4.25:1. Overall gear ratios 4.25, 5.70, 8.58, 12.67, reverse 13.42:1. RR-General Motors Hydramatic 4-speed automatic transmission on two cars (and two others later converted). Overall ratios 4.25, 6.16, 11.18, 16.23, reverse 18.27:1.

Suspension and brakes: Ifs, coil springs, wishbones, anti-roll bar and lever-arm hydraulic dampers; live rear axle, half-elliptic leaf springs and adjustable (by driver's lever control) lever-arm hydraulic dampers. Cam-and-roller steering, 3.5 turns lock-to-lock. 12.25 × 2.6in diameter front and rear drum brakes, with mechanical servo assistance (servo mounted on transmission). 7.00-17in cross-ply tyres on 5in-rimmed steel disc wheels.
Dimensions: Wheelbase 12ft 1in (368.3cm); front track 4ft 10.5in (148.6cm); rear track 5ft 3in (160cm). Depending on coachwork fitted, overall length about 18ft 11in (576.6cm); width 6ft 5in (195.6cm); height 6ft 2in (188cm). Unladen weight about 3,300lb (chassis only), or about 5,000lb (complete car).
Basic price when introduced in 1950: Car never available for general sale.

Rolls-Royce Phantom V — produced 1959 to 1968
Engine: V8-cyl, with overhead inlet and exhaust valves, 104.1 × 91.4mm, 6,230cc (4.09 × 3.59in, 380cu in), CR 8.0:1. Twin horizontal constant-vacuum SU carbs. Peak power never officially revealed, but estimated at approx 200bhp (nett) at 4,000rpm.
Transmission: Manual transmission not available. All cars built with RR-General Motors 4-speed automatic transmission, incorporating a fluid flywheel. Rear axle ratio 3.89:1. Overall gear ratios 3.89, 5.64, 10.23, 14.86, reverse 16.72:1. 22.5mph/1,000rpm in top gear.
Suspension: Ifs, coil springs, wishbones, anti-roll bar and lever-arm hydraulic dampers: live rear-axle, half-elliptic leaf springs and adjustable lever-arm hydraulic dampers. Cam-and-roller steering, 4.25 turns lock-to-lock, with power assistance. 11.25 × 3in diameter front and rear drum brakes, with mechanical servo assistance. 8.90-15in cross-ply tyres on 6in-rimmed steel disc wheels.
Dimensions: Wheelbase 12ft 1in (368.3cm); front track 5ft 0.9in (154.6cm); rear track 5ft 4in (162.6cm). Note: The wheelbase is often misquoted at 12ft 0in but has always been 12ft 1in. Depending on coachwork fitted, overall length about 19ft 10in (624cm); width 6ft 7in (200.6cm); height 5ft 9in (175.3cm). These dimensions apply to the most numerous limousine coachwork, by H.J. Mulliner, Park Ward. A good proportion of cars, however, were bodied by James Young until 1967-68. Unladen weight about 5,600lb (2,540kg).
Basic price when introduced in 1959: £6,285 for H.J. Mulliner, Park Ward limousine, approximately £6,700 for alternative styles — plus extras!
Development changes: For 1963, the Phantom V received a more powerful engine, as did other models, with CR 9:1 (except for certain export markets). Power, as ever, was not stated, but is estimated at approx 220bhp (nett) at 4,000rpm.
By 1967, the last alternative coachbuilt style to the 'standard' H.J. Mulliner, Park Ward limousine had gone, with the closure of the James Young business.

Rolls-Royce Phantom VI — produced 1968 to date
Basic specification as for late-model Phantom Vs until spring 1978, except for standardization of front and rear refrigeration. Two standard body styles — the H.J. Mulliner, Park Ward limousine and (to special order) the H.J. Mulliner, Park Ward landaulette — were still available.
Basic kerbside weight had risen to approximately 6,000lb (2,721kg).
Development changes: From the spring of 1978, starting with the motor industry's 'gift' car to H.M. The Queen on the occasion of her Silver Jubilee, the following mechanical changes were made:
Engine: 104.1 × 99.1mm, 6,750cc (4.09 × 3.90in, 411.9cu in). Power output not quoted but approx 200 bhp.
Transmission: GM Type GM400 automatic transmission. Rear axle ratio 3.89:1 (as before). Overall gear ratios 3.89, 5.757, 9.647, reverse 8.091:1, with torque converter; maximum torque multiplication 2.0:1.
Suspension: Drum brakes now operated by high-pressure hydraulics (Silver Shadow-type).
Basic price: Phantom VI, on announcement in October 1968: £10,050. The basic price of the 6.7-litre Phantom VI has never been disclosed, being 'on application'. In 1984, prices started at £100,000.

Bentley R-Type Continental — produced 1952 to 1955
Engine: 6-cylinder, overhead inlet, side exhaust valves, 92.1 × 114.3mm, 4,566cc (3.625 × 4.5in, 278.6cu in), CR 7.27:1 (at first, later 7.1 or 7.2:1). Twin horizontal constant-vacuum SU carbs. Peak power never officially revealed. Transmission: 11in single-dry-plate clutch, and four-speed manual gearbox, with no synchromesh on first gear. Rear axle ratio 3.077:1. Overall gear ratios 3.077, 3.741, 4.750, 8.222, reverse 8.802:1. 27.0mph/1,000rpm in top gear.
Suspension and brakes: Ifs, coil springs, wishbones, anti-roll bar and lever-arm hydraulic dampers; live rear axle, half-elliptic leaf springs and adjustable lever-arm hydraulic dampers. Cam-and-roller steering, 3.6 turns lock-to-lock. 12.25 × 2.25in front and rear drum brakes, with mechanical servo assistance. 6.50-16in cross-ply tyres on 5in-rimmed steel disc wheels.
Dimensions: Wheelbase 10ft 0in (304.8cm); front track 4ft 8.5in (143.5cm); rear track 4ft 10.5in (148.6cm). Depending on coachwork fitted (dimensions for Mulliner two-door coupe style), overall length about 17ft 2.5in (524.5cm); width 5ft 11.5in (181.6cm); height 5ft 3in (160cm). Unladen weight (depending on coachwork) about 3,700lb (1,678kg).
Basic price when introduced in 1952: £4,890 (export only at first).
Development changes: 4-speed Rolls-Royce/GM Hydramatic automatic transmission, with fluid flywheel, was announced in

autumn 1952 for all Rolls-Royce and Bentley models, but was not available in the R-Type Continental until the enlarged engine was also phased in.

From mid-1954, the car's specification was altered as follows:Engine: 95.25 × 114.3mm, 4,887cc (3.75 × 4.5in, 298.2cu in); CR 7.25:1.

Transmission: Optional RR/GM Hydramatic 4-speed automatic transmission with fluid flywheel. Overall gear ratios 3.077, 4.290, 8.070, 11.720, reverse 13.410:1. Unladen weight, depending on coachwork fitted, from about 3,800lb (1,723kg). Basic price when introduced in 1954: £4,890 for H.J. Mulliner body style.

Bentley S1 Continental — produced 1955 to 1959

Engine: 6-cyl, overhead inlet and side exhaust valves, 95.25 × 114.3mm, 4,887cc (3.75 × 4.5in, 298.2cu in), CR 7.25:1, 8:1 from autumn 1956. Twin horizontal constant-vacuum SU carbs. Peak power never officially revealed, but with 8:1 compression estimated at 178bhp (nett) at 4,000rpm.

Transmission: Automatic transmission as standard, but manual transmission to special order on first few cars. Rear axle ratio in each case 2.923:1. Overall gear ratios (manual) 2.923, 3.554, 4.501, 7.804, reverse 8.363: 1. Overall gear ratios (automatic) 2.923, 4.25, 7.69, 11.17, reverse 12.59:1. 28.4mph/1,000rpm in top gear.

Suspension and brakes: Ifs, coil springs, wishbones, anti-roll bar and lever-arm hydraulic dampers; live rear axle, half-elliptic leaf springs, 'Z-bar' acting as radius aam/anti-roll device, and adjustable lever-arm hydraulic dampers. Cam-and-roller steering, 4.25 turns lock-to-lock, no power assistance at first, optional on some models from spring 1956 (export only), on all models from autumn 1956. 11.25 × 3in front and rear drum brakes, with mechanical servo assistance. 7.60-15in cross-ply tyres (later changed to 8.00-15in) on 6in-rimmed steel disc wheels.

Dimensions: Wheelbase 10ft 3in (312.4cm); front track 4ft 10in (147.3cm); rear track 5ft 0in (152.4cm). Depending on coachwork fitted (dimensions for popular H.J. Mulliner style), overall length about 17ft 8in (539.5cm); width 5ft 11.5in (181.6cm); height 5ft 4in (162.6cm). Unladen weight (depending on coachwork) about 4,255lb (1,930kg).

Basic price when introduced in 1955: S1 Continental chassis £2,510, typical complete price (H.J. Mulliner) £4,960.

Bentley S2 Continental — produced 1959 to 1962

Basic specification as for S1 Continental models except for:
Engine: V8-cyl, with overhead inlet and exhaust valves, 104.1 × 91.4mm, 6,230cc (4.09 × 3.59in, 380cu in), CR 8:1. Twin horizontal constant-vacuum SU carbs. Peak power never officially revealed, but estimated at approx 200bhp (nett) at 4,000rpm.
Transmission: Manual transmission not available on any cars.

Dimensions: Front track 4ft 10.5in (148.6cm). Unladen weight (depending on coachwork) from 4,225lb (1,930kg).
Basic price when introduced in 1959: S2 Continental chassis £2,935, typical complete price (H.J. Mulliner 2-door, or Flying Spur 4-door) £5,730.

Bentley S3 Continental — produced 1962 to 1965

Basic specification as for S2 models, except for:
Engine: CR 9:1 (except CR 8:1 for certain export markets). Peak power estimated at approx 220bhp (nett) at 4,000rpm with 9:1 CR.
Basic price when introduced in 1962: S3 Continental chassis £3,080, typical complete price (H.J. Mulliner 2-door or Flying Spur 4-door) £6,505.

From 1957 to 1965, Rolls-Royce also offered a long-wheelbase version of the S-Series 'standard-steel' saloon bodyshell with a limousine division, produced as a conversion by Park Ward. Styling was virtually the same as the standard model, except for different rear quarter-window profiles, and the specifications were as follows:

Rolls-Royce Silver Cloud I and Bentley S1 long-wheelbase limousine — produced 1957 to 1959

Specification as for 'standard-steel' saloons (see Volume 1), except for:
Dimensions: Wheelbase 10ft 7in (322.6cm). Overall length 17ft 11.7in (548cm). Unladen weight 4,650lb (2,109kg).
Basic price when introduced in 1957: Rolls-Royce version £4,595, Bentley version £4,595.

Rolls-Royce Silver Cloud II and Bentley S2 long-wheelbase limousines — produced 1959 to 1962

Specification as for 'standard-steel' saloons (see Volume 1), except for:
Dimensions: Wheelbase 10ft 7in (322.6cm). Overall length 17ft 11.7in (548cm). Unladen weight 4,815lb (2,184kg).
Basic price when introduced in 1959: Rolls-Royce version £4,995, Bentley version £4,900.

Rolls-Royce Silver Cloud III and Bentley S3 long-wheelbase limousines — produced 1962 to 1966

Specification as for 'standard-steel' saloons (see Volume 1), except for:
Dimensions: Wheelbase 10ft 7in (322.6cm). Overall length 17ft 11.7in (548cm). Unladen weight 4,815lb (2,184kg).
Basic price when introduced in 1962: Rolls-Royce version £5,570, Bentley version £5,465.

Note: Special coachwork was also available on all the above long-wheelbase models.

APPENDIX B

Chassis identification

Identification of any postwar Rolls-Royce or Bentley can always be precise, even when the coachbuilt bodyshell is an individual design and may have been added to the car in an overseas territory. Not only is this because each car was allocated a 'chassis card' from the moment that its existence was confirmed, but because each and every one of these cards has been preserved. The identity of every car, *except* the Phantom VI models, built in the period covered in this book is already assured, because all the chassis cards, and a great deal more detail about the individual cars, are held in the meticulous hands of the Sir Henry Royce Memorial Foundation, a charitable organization set up by members of the Rolls-Royce Enthusiasts' Club. The Phantom VI cards are still held by Rolls-Royce Motors Ltd, at Crewe, but will be handed over one day, no doubt.

However, while it is easy enough to quote the chassis numbers of all the coachbuilt cars, it is by no means short, or simple. Throughout the period covered, Rolls-Royce identified their cars by sequences of numbers and letters, changing these sequences frequently, sometimes after only a few cars had been built. To make it all the more fascinating and complex to understand, I should also point out that alternate numbers, not consecutive numbers, were sometimes used, sometimes odd, but sometimes even, and that no car carried the chassis number 13. All left-hand-drive cars carried the chassis prefix 'L' — *i.e.* LWSG53 for a Silver Wraith.

Cars from the 'standard-steel' chassis range of Rolls-Royces or Bentleys, on the standard-length wheelbase, took chassis from the normal 'standard-steel' sequences, but long-wheelbase versions of those cars had their own special sequences.

After that preamble, here are the details for each model:

Rolls-Royce Silver Wraith (1946-1959)

WTA1 — WTA85	Note: Chassis numbers for Silver Wraiths were consecutive — *i.e.* odd numbers *and* even numbers were used)

WVA1 — WVA81	WDC1 — WDC101
WYA1 — WYA87	WFC1 — WFC101
WZB1 — WZB65	WGC1 — WGC101
WAB1 — WAB65	WHD1 — WHD101
WCB1 — WCB73	WLE1 — WLE35
WME1 — WME96 (Last cars with 4¼-litre engine)	
WOF1 — WOF76 (First cars with 4½-litre engine)	
WSG1 — WSG76 (LWSG53 first car with automatic transmission)	

WVH1 — WVH116	
ALW1 — ALW51	(Wheelbase increased by 6 inches)
BLW1 — BLW101	
CLW1 — CLW43	(Last cars with 4½-litre engine)
DLW1 — DLW166	(First cars with 4.9-litre engine)
ELW1 — ELW101	
FLW1 — FLW101	(First cars with SU carburettor engine)
GLW1 — GLW26	
HLW1 — HLW52	(Last chassis delivery in October 1958, last car delivery in August 1959)

Note: The chassis of the first long-wheelbase car (133in instead of 127in) was built in July 1951 (but completed car not delivered until January 1952). All long-wheelbase Silver Wraiths had a chassis number sequence including the letters 'LW' — *i.e.* all cars from ALW1 to HLW52.

Rolls-Royce Phantom IV (1950-1956)

4AF2 — 4AF22	Even numbers
4BP1 — 4BP7	Odd numbers
4CS2 — 4CS6	Even numbers (Last chassis built in December 1955, last complete car delivered in November 1956)

All Phantom IVs were built on the same 145in wheelbase; 2 of them were built with automatic transmission from new and 2 others were later converted to automatic from manual.

Rolls-Royce Silver Dawn (1949-1955)

Mechanically, coachbuilt examples of the Silver Dawn were identical with the 'standard-steel' cars and carried chassis numbers from those sequences. However, in 6 years, a total of 66 special coachbuilt Silver Dawns were built.

Rolls-Royce Phantom V (1959-1968)

5AS1 — 5AS101	Odds
5AT2 — 5AT100	Evens
5BV1 — 5BV101	Odds
5BX2 — 5BX100	Evens
5CG1 — 5CG79	Odds
5VA1 — 5VA123	All numbers (First 9:1 CR engines used)
5VB1 — 5VB51	All numbers
5VC1 — 5VC51	All numbers
5VD1 — 5VD101	All numbers
5VE1 — 5VE51	All numbers
5VF1 — 5VF183	All numbers (Last chassis built February 1968, last car delivered in June 1968)

Note: The 2 high-roof 'Canberra' Phantom Vs for H.M. The Queen were 5AS33 and 5AT34, respectively.

A total of 9 landaulette bodies of 2 sub-types were built on this chassis.

Rolls-Royce Silver Cloud SI, SII and SIII (1955-1966)

Mechanically, coachbuilt examples of the standard-wheelbase Silver Clouds were identical with the 'standard-steel' cars and carried chassis numbers in those sequences. It has not proved practical to check every chassis card for the numbers involved, but the total 11-year quantity is estimated at less than 130 cars in all.

Rolls-Royce Silver Cloud SI long-wheelbase (1957-1959)

ALC1 — ALC26	All numbers
BLC1 — BLC51	All numbers
CLC1 — CLC47	All numbers (Last car delivered in August 1959)

Rolls-Royce Silver Cloud SII long-wheelbase (1959-1962)

LCA1 — LCA76	All numbers
LCB1 — LCB101	All numbers
LCC1 — LCC101	All numbers
LCD1 — LCD25	All numbers (Last car delivered in September 1962)

Rolls-Royce Silver Cloud SIII long-wheelbase (1962-1965)

CAL1 — CAL83	All SIII long-wheelbase cars had *odd* chassis numbers
CBL1 — CBL61	
CCL1 — CCL101	
CDL1 — CDL95	
CEL1 — CEL105	
CFL1 — CFL41	
CGL1 — CGL27	(Last car delivered in October 1965)

Rolls-Royce Phantom VI (1968 to the present)

Starting from mid-1968, when the Phantom VI took over from the Phantom V, a new standardized chassis lettering sequence was adopted. This was PRH (right-hand-drive)/PRX (left-hand-drive), having much in common with Silver Shadows, T-Series Bentleys and other derivatives. The code is 'cracked' as follows:

P = Phantom VI
R = Rolls-Royce
H = Right-hand-drive (or Home specification)
X = Left-hand-drive (or Export specification)

The original Phantom VI was PRH4108, and a further handful of cars were delivered, interspersed with normal Silver Shadow/T-Series numbers in the 4100-4505 range, before a special consecutive run of numbers was allocated. These were:

PRH 4503
PRH 4504
PRH 4549 — PRX 4874 All numbers, except the 4670 to 4699 were never used.

The car was then redesigned to have the 6.75-litre engine, the GM400 3-speed/torque converter automatic gearbox and Silver Shadow-type high-pressure hydraulic operation of the braking system. A new chassis sequence, quite separate from the Shadow/T-Series sequence, was initiated and continues at the time of writing:

PGH101 — This was the special high-roofed car, dubbed 'Canberra 3', presented to H.M. The Queen as a Silver Jubilee gift by the SMM&T. The style is like that of 'Canberra 1' and 'Canberra 2'. It was delivered in March 1978.

PGH102 — PGH134 All numbers, starting in the spring of 1978.

These cars, like all others in Western Europe, were then given new, complex and lengthy VIN (Vehicle Identification Numbers), but very few have been built so far.

At the time of preparing this Appendix, in mid-1984, a total of 5 6.23-litre Phantom VI landaulettes and just 2 6.75-litre landaulettes had been built. Almost every other car had the 'standard' H.J. Mulliner, Park Ward 7-seat limousine body style, but 2 cars were supplied 'chassis only', to be bodied by Frua. One of these, shown at the 1973 Frankfurt motor show, was a vast convertible.

Bentley Mk VI and R-Type (1946-1955)

Mechanically, coachbuilt examples of the Mk VI and R-Type were identical with the 'standard-steel' cars and carried chassis numbers from those sequences. However, in 9 years, a total of 820 4¼-litre Mk VI, 179 4½-litre Mk VI and 303 R-Type special coachbuilt Bentleys were built.

Bentley S1 long-wheelbase (1957-1959)

ALB1 — ALB36	All numbers (Last car delivered July 1959)

Bentley S2 long-wheelbase (1959-1962)

LBA1 — LBA26	All numbers
LBB1 — LBB33	All numbers (Last car delivered August 1962)

Bentley S3 long-wheelbase (1962-1965)

BAL2 — BAL30	Even numbers
BBL2 — BBL12	Even numbers
BCL2 — BCL22	Even numbers (Last car delivered September 1965)

Bentley R-Type Continental (1952-1955)

BC1A — BC26A	All numbers
BC1B — BC25B	
BC1C — BC78C	(First cars fitted with automatic transmission)
BC1D — BC74D	(Engine size increased to 4.9 litres)
BC1E — BC9E	(Last car delivered May 1955)

Of the 208 cars, no fewer than 193 were fitted with the 'standard' H J. Mulliner sports saloon coachwork — with Park Ward, Franay, Graber and Farina sharing the other 15 chassis. See main text for details.

Bentley S1 Continental (1955-1959)
BC1AF — BC102AF   All numbers
BC1BG — BC101BG
BC1CH — BC51CH
BC1DJ — BC51DJ
BC1EL — BC51EL
BC1FM — BC51FM
BC1GN — BC31GN   (Last car delivered December 1960)
   All but 28 chassis were clothed by H.J. Mulliner (218 cars) or Park Ward (185 cars). James Young (20), Hooper (6), Graber and Franay (a single car each) shared the rest.

Bentley S2 Continental (1959-1962)
BC1AR — BC151AR   All numbers

BC1BY — BC101BY
BC1CZ — BC139CZ   (Last car delivered October 1962)
   H.J. Mulliner (221), Park Ward (125), James Young (41) and Hooper (a single car) supplied the coachwork.

Bentley S3 Continental (1962-1966)
BC2XA — BC174XA   All S3 Continentals used *even* numbers
BC2XB — BC100XB
BC2XC — BC202XC
BC2XD — BC28XD
BC2XE — BC120XE   (Last car delivered January 1966)
   H.J. Mulliner, Park Ward (the merged concern — 75), H.J. Mulliner (68), Park Ward (148), James Young (20) and Graber (a single car) supplied the coachwork.

APPENDIX C

Production and deliveries — 1946 to 1984

A careful count and cross-check of the available Rolls-Royce and Bentley chassis cards allows accurate production statistics of coachbuilt models to be presented here. However, I have only quoted total production of each type, rather than annual production as well. This is because there was always a lengthy delay (months, sometimes more than a year) between the date of delivery of the rolling chassis from Rolls-Royce to the coachbuilder, and delivery of the completed car to the customer (in the UK), or to the docks for overseas shipment. That way, at least, I have avoided a lot of tedious explanation and bets-hedging!

Here are the details:

Rolls-Royce Silver Wraith (127in wheelbase)	1,144
Rolls-Royce Silver Wraith (133in wheelbase)	639
Rolls-Royce Phantom IV (see text)	18
Rolls-Royce Phantom V	793
Rolls-Royce Phantom VI (6¼-litre engine)	311
Rolls-Royce Phantom VI (6¾-litre engine)	n/a**
Bentley R-Type Continental	208
(this total includes 82 4.9-litre cars)	
Bentley S1 Continental	431
Bentley S2 Continental	388
Bentley S3 Continental	312
Rolls-Royce Silver Cloud I long-wheelbase (standard body style)	85
Rolls-Royce Silver Cloud I long-wheelbase (special coachwork)	36
Bentley S1 long-wheelbase (standard body style)	23
Bentley S1 long-wheelbase (special coachwork)	12
Rolls-Royce Silver Cloud II long-wheelbase (standard body style)	258
Rolls-Royce Silver Cloud II long-wheelbase (special coachwork)	41
Bentley S2 long-wheelbase (standard body style)	51
Bentley S2 long-wheelbase (special coachwork)	6
Rolls-Royce Silver Cloud III long-wheelbase (standard body style)	206
Rolls-Royce Silver Cloud III long-wheelbase (special coachwork)	47
Bentley S3 long-wheelbase (standard body style)	25
Bentley S3 long-wheelbase (special coachwork)	7

In addition, the 'standard-steel' chassis was provided to coachbuilders for special coachwork to be added. In the early postwar years this represented a significant proportion of the business, but quantities declined dramatically with the advent of the Silver Cloud/S-Series cars.

While it has not been practical to search out the odd 1 or 2 coachbuilt cars in the Silver Cloud chassis cards, other statistics are as follows:

Bentley Mk VI (4¼-litre) (special coachwork)	820
Bentley Mk VI (4½-litre) (special coachwork)	179

Bentley R-Type (special coachwork)	303
Rolls-Royce Silver Dawn (special coachwork)	66
Bentley S1(special coachwork)	145
Bentley S2(special coachwork)	15
Bentley S3 (special coachwork)	2

In the first 3 years of Silver Cloud production, for instance, 88 cars were supplied with special coachwork and demand had virtually dried up by then.

**Production of 6¾-litre Phantom VI models has always been at a very low rate, latterly even lower than 10 cars a year. By mid-1984, therefore, production of this derivative was still only of the order of 50 cars.

APPENDIX D

How fast? How thirsty? How heavy? Performance figures for selected coachbuilt models

There were far too many variables in this type and category of Rolls-Royce or Bentley for the performance figures quoted to provide a full story covering nearly 40 years, but at least they give a flavour.

In the case of the big limousines, Rolls-Royce Ltd rarely thought it necessary for their performance to be measured. Like the unquoted power output of the engines, this was always thought to be 'adequate'. A diligent search through the files of *Autocar* and *Motor* has turned up only two full factual tests — a magnificent Silver Wraith tested by *The Autocar* in 1949 and a Phantom V by *The Motor* in 1962.

Of the Silver Wraith, *the Autocar* wrote: 'The charm, the appeal, the true practical worth of this car among other cars is not that it has the highest performance capable of being derived from 4¼ litres of six-cylinder engine designed and built in the Rolls-Royce manner, a phrase meaning so much, but as so often has been said, the way in which the car behaves and handles . . .', which sums up the necessary approach to performance of these cars.

With the Bentley Continentals, of course, it is a different story, for great attempts were always made to endow these cars with formidable performance by the standards of the day. *The Autocar* tested three distinctly different types of Continental in eight years, and a comparison is illuminating:

	Rolls-Royce Silver Wraith Sedanca de Ville (H.J. Mulliner 4-dr/7-seat) 6-cyl 4,257cc (Manual)	Rolls-Royce Phantom V Limousine (Park Ward 4-dr/7-seat) V8-cyl 6,230cc (Auto)	Bentley Continental Coupe R-Type (H.J. Mulliner 2-dr/4-seat) 6-cyl 4,566cc (Manual)	Bentley Continental DHC S-Type (Park Ward 2-dr/4-seat) 6-cyl 4,887cc (Auto)	Bentley Continental Saloon S-Type (James Young 4-dr/4-seat) V8-cyl 6,230 (Auto)
Maximum speed (mph)	n.a.*	101	115	119	113
Acceleration (sec)					
0-30mph	7.9	4.1	4.4	4.3	4.0
0-40mph	-	6.6	-	-	6.3
0-50mph	17.2	9.7	10.5	9.3	8.9
0-60mph	24.0	13.8	13.5	12.9	12.1
0-70mph	37.4	19.3	16.3	17.1	15.9
0-80mph	-	26.5	22.2	21.3	20.5
0-90mph	-	36.0	28.1	29.5	26.9
0-100mph	-	-	36.0	40.2	37.1
Standing ¼-mile (sec)	-	19.4	19.5	18.8	18.6

	Rolls-Royce Silver Wraith Sedanca de Ville (H.J. Mulliner 4-dr/7-seat) 6-cyl 4,257cc (Manual)	Rolls-Royce Phantom V Limousine (Park Ward 4-dr/7-seat) V8-cyl 6,230cc (Auto) **	Bentley Continental Coupe R-Type (H.J. Mulliner 2-dr/4-seat) 6-cyl 4,566cc (Manual) **	Bentley Continental DHC S-Type (Park Ward 2-dr/4-seat) 6-cyl 4,887cc (Auto)	Bentley Continental Saloon S-Type (James Young 4-dr/4-seat) V8-cyl 6,230 (Auto)
Direct top gear (sec)					
10-30mph	13.5	3.0	8.2	2.9	-
20-40mph	12.4	4.3	7.4	4.0	-
30-50mph	13.0	5.6	7.4	5.2	7.6
40-60mph	-	7.2	7.4	6.6	7.8
50-70mph	-	9.6	8.4	7.3	8.7
60-80mph	-	12.7	9.6	8.4	10.2
70-90mph	-	16.7	12.1	12.2	12.2
80-100mph	-	-	14.6	17.9	16.6
Overall fuel consumption (mpg)	15-17	11.1	19.4	15.2	13.1
Typical fuel consumption (mpg)	17	13	21	18	17
Kerb weight (lb)	4,732	5,712	3,739	3,976	4,460
Original test published	1949	1962	1952	1956	1960

Note: All tests by *The Autocar,* except for the Phantom V test, which was by *The Motor.*

*Maximum speed not measured — estimated to be approx 85mph.

**Denotes figures taken in 'kickdown' of the automatic transmission. Other tests of automatic-transmission cars were 'figured' with the use of kickdown avoided.

Notes:
One significant feature is the way that the weight of Rolls-Royce limousines increased over the years, for the original Phantom V was no less than 980lb/444kg heavier than the Silver Wraith of the late 1940s. That was not the end of it, for I understand that a later model Phantom VI, complete with separate refrigeration plants and more equipment than ever, can scale in excess of 6,000lb/2,721kg, and one of the very rare landaulettes even more!

The fascinating point about Bentley Continentals is that the late models with the V8 engine were really no quicker than the original sleek 4¼-litre-engined cars, this partly being due to an increase in weight (721lb/327kg) in less than a decade, and partly to the much larger frontal area and less aerodynamic shape of the later models.

The overall fuel consumption figures — 19.4mpg in 1952, but a mere 13.1mpg in 1960, tell their own story. The S2 test car's final-drive ratio was 3.08:1, not 2.92 as was usual for Continentals. This may explain the rather disappointing top speed.

As with the 'standard-steel' models described in the companion volume, it is difficult to make valid comparisons between cars in regard to top-gear performance, especially as three of the five cars had automatic transmission, and two of those were tested by using the kickdown, while the other was tested with kickdown being scrupulously avoided. (In 'kickdown', of course, the automatic transmission changes down to a lower ratio below certain engine load and road speed points.)